Gun Control
The Pros and Cons

Tom Streissguth

Enslow Publishers, Inc.

40 Industrial Road   PO Box 38
Box 398   Aldershot
Berkeley Heights, NJ 07922 Hants GU12 6BP
USA   UK

http://www.enslow.com

Library of Congress Cataloging-in-Publication Data

Streissguth, Thomas, 1958–
     Gun control : the pros and cons / Tom Streissguth.
          p. cm. — (Issues in focus)
     Includes bibliographical references and index.
     ISBN 0-7660-1673-0 (hbk.)
     1. Firearms—Law and legislation—United States—Juvenile
literature. 2. Gun control—United States—Juvenile literature.
[1. Gun control. 2. Firearms—Law and legislation.] I. Title.
II. Issues in focus
     (Hillside, N.J.)
     KF3942.H3 S77 2001
     344.73'0533—dc211
                                                        00-012171

Printed in the United States of America

10 9 8 7 6 5 4 3 2

To Our Readers:
We have done our best to make sure all Internet addresses in this book
were active and appropriate when we went to press. However, the author
and publisher have no control over and assume no liability for the
material available on those Internet sites or on other Web sites they
may link to. Any comments or suggestions can be sent by e-mail to
comments@enslow.com or to the address on the back cover.

Illustration Credits: Brown Brothers, p. 23; Enslow Publishers, Inc.,
pp. 66, 67, 70, 71, 86, 87; courtesy of Francha Roffé Menhard, pp. 8,
13, 63, 93; Library of Congress, pp. 11, 22; Library of Congress/Acme
Newspictures, Inc., p. 24; Library of Congress/Associated Press, p. 34;
Library of Congress/Civil War Photograph Collection, p. 20; Library of
Congress/Joseph H. Green, pp. 18, 21; Library of Congress/*New York
World-Telegram* and the Sun Newspaper Photograph Collection, p. 37;
Library of Congress/Painting by Henry Sandham, p. 16; Library of
Congress/Portrait of America Collection, p. 35; National Archives, p. 48.

Cover Illustration: Corbis Images Royalty-Free.

Contents

1

The Rampage

Richard Scott Baumhammers lived near Pittsburgh, Pennsylvania. He worked as an immigration lawyer, but he opposed immigration. He was against Hispanics, Africans, Asians, and other nonwhite people coming to the United States. He had even formed his own political party, the Free Market Party. Like all other citizens, Baumhammers had a right to write, speak, and vote for what he believed in. The First Amendment to the U.S. Constitution guarantees the right to practice religion and express opinions.

But Baumhammers did not stop with a

5

new political party. He decided to kill as well. His rampage took place on Friday, April 28, 2000, in Mount Lebanon, Pennsylvania. He began by setting his neighbor's house on fire. Using a .357 Magnum, a powerful handgun, he then shot the elderly Jewish woman who lived there.

Baumhammers roamed through the suburbs of Pittsburgh from one town to the next. He stopped in shopping malls and picked out people with features and skin color different from his. He shot one man at a grocery, two more in a Chinese restaurant, and a fifth victim at a karate school. He then fired at the Beth El Congregation synagogue, where Jewish worshippers gathered for services.

Another Important Amendment

Rage against foreigners or against those appearing different did not begin with Baumhammers. Nor is it restricted to white people. Just two months earlier, Ronald Taylor, an African American, shot and killed three white men in Wilkinsburg, another Pittsburgh suburb.

To express their anger, Baumhammers and Taylor used handguns. They also used an important constitutional amendment: the Second. The Second Amendment mentions the importance of militias, or civilian military groups. According to the Constitution, militias are so important to freedom that the people of the United States have a natural right to keep and bear arms.

An Incident of Self-Protection

The shooting spree by Baumhammers took place in the early months of the year 2000 presidential campaign, with Republican George W. Bush running against Democrat Al Gore. During this campaign, the candidates paid close attention to the issue of guns and violence. The argument over gun control had been especially intense since April 1999. In that month, Dylan Klebold and Eric Harris went on a rampage at Columbine High School in Littleton, Colorado. The two students used guns sold to them by adults to kill more than a dozen other students and then themselves.

Over the following year, several more shooting sprees took place. The shock of the Columbine tragedy wore away, but the controversy over guns remained. The nation's attention returned to the issue in February 2000, when a six-year-old boy shot and killed Kayla Rolland, one of his first-grade classmates at Buell Elementary School in Mount Morris, Michigan.

The tragic shootings led to new proposals in the United States Congress, where federal laws are made. A new juvenile justice bill was proposed. The law would have required special "trigger locks" that can only be opened by the gun-owner's key. It would also have required background checks on people buying weapons at gun shows. With a background check, the seller of a gun can find out if the buyer has a criminal record—and so cannot legally buy a gun.

Many voters strongly supported the bill—and

Two students at Columbine High School in Colorado read the memorial poster for the students who were killed in the 1999 shooting by two of their fellow students. The students, Dylan Klebold and Eric Harris, fatally shot themselves after they murdered thirteen people.

many others strongly opposed it. The members of Congress argued long and loud about gun control. Supporters and opponents could not reach a compromise. The juvenile justice bill did not pass.

Gun Control—Pro and Con

Those favoring more restrictions on guns pointed to the Columbine massacre and other shootings to support their position. They believe there are too many guns in the United States. The Columbine killers bought their weapons easily enough, even though they were not old enough, legally, to buy or carry them. Instead of going through a licensed dealer or gun store, the teens bought three of their weapons from an adult. The adult had made a "straw purchase," purchasing the weapons at a gun show, then turning the guns over to the real buyers.

In an article in *salon.com* magazine entitled "The Real Culprits at Columbine," the writer partially blames the killings on the most powerful association opposing gun-control laws, the National Rifle Association (NRA):

> The National Rifle Association and its powerful allies argue that Klebold and Harris broke a dozen or so gun laws that day they jumped into the headlines and sadly, became the story of 1999. More laws aren't the answer, the NRA says. Enforce the ones that exist. . . .
>
> Clearly, more went wrong at Columbine High School than just a lack of gun laws. There were police screw ups, inattentive parents,

nefarious entertainment influences. But none of that means that tougher gun laws couldn't have prevented the tragedy. Or at least set up a few roadblocks.[1]

Those opposed to gun control support their position with other news stories. On August 19, 1999, in Covington, Kentucky, Jamie Kennedy approached Joe Megerle in Covington's Devou Park. Kennedy pulled out an unloaded gun, pointed it at Megerle, and demanded money. Megerle pulled out a gun of his own and shot Kennedy in the head and in the chest. Megerle had applied for and received a permit that allowed him to carry a concealed handgun.

Kentucky legislators passed SB17, also known as the "concealed-carry" law, in 1996. More than 51,000 state residents obtained permits during the next three years. Gun-control opponents support such laws. They believe that concealed-carry laws stop violent crime—in a concealed-carry state, criminals cannot be sure whether or not their victims are armed because they may not see a gun. After the shooting in Covington, Sheriff Charles Korzenborn of Kenton County, said, "People have not only a right but a responsibility to take care of themselves . . . If you rely on the police to do everything, you would need one policeman for every person."[2]

Arguing About the Second Amendment

The Second Amendment to the United States Constitution forms the basis of the gun-control controversy. The first ten amendments to the U.S. Constitution are known as the Bill of Rights. The

Second Amendment deals with the right of citizens to own firearms. It reads: "A well-regulated militia, being necessary to the security of a free state, the right of the people to keep and bear arms shall not be infringed."

Around this single sentence swirls an old controversy over the proper role of firearms. Those who oppose gun control claim the Second Amendment means that citizens have a right to own as many guns as they want. Gun-control opponents also understand the amendment as a guarantee of personal liberty. They believe that armed citizens can resist tyranny, while those living under restrictive gun-control laws risk allowing a totalitarian government to take power.

Those favoring gun control see the amend-ment differently. They say that it refers to armed forces made up of private citizens (militias), not necessarily individuals. They claim that the amendment was passed

James Madison, author of the Bill of Rights, made the right to bear arms into a constitutional guarantee. But the meaning of his words in the Second Amendment is still the subject of intense debate.

in a very different time, when such militias fought for independence from England. They see the right to bear arms as a collective right, which belongs to the public in general. They believe that "well-regulated" means that the Bill of Rights allows reasonable laws controlling guns.

The debate has not been resolved, despite many years of Supreme Court cases (in which the Constitution is interpreted), authoritative articles, new history books, new laws, and many debates in the U.S. Congress. In his book on the gun industry, *Making a Killing*, Tom Diaz sums up the great divide separating pro- and anti-gun forces:

> Few things arouse as much visceral passion among Americans as firearms do. To many, guns are repulsive and exceedingly dangerous, even evil. But to others, guns are venerated objects of craftsmanship and tangible symbols of such fundamental American values as independence, self-reliance, and freedom from governmental interference. This divide has made the national debate about firearms often seem to be a shouting match between people from different planets—or at least from different eras—talking about entirely different things.[3]

The Modern Debate

Gun ownership has remained high in the United States, where about half of all households include people who own at least one gun. By the mid-1990s, there were some 67 million handguns, 73 million rifles, and 63 million shotguns—about one firearm for every individual in the nation. Gun ownership had reached 25 percent of all households in the Midwest, 18 percent in the West, 13 percent in the Northeast, and 44 percent in the South.[4]

Pro-gun and anti-gun citizens agree on a few things. They both understand that gun ownership is higher in the United States than it is in most other countries. They realize there are many more deaths and injuries caused by guns here than in foreign countries. They also know about the violent history of the United States. They agree that guns and violence have been important in American life, and in American books, movies, and television, for a long

Guns have become a commonplace in American life.

time. Violence is also a huge factor in computer games.

Yet the two sides see the same story in a different light. Those who favor gun control believe that guns no longer guarantee liberty and are not needed for the taming of a nonexistent frontier. Instead, they see guns—especially handguns—as the cause of fatal accidents, tragic suicides, and violent crime in the modern world. Most gun-control supporters believe that handguns should be tightly controlled or banned altogether.

Opponents of gun control believe that guns still guarantee our liberties. They see gun-control laws as a threat to the personal freedom of Americans. They do not want to see handguns banned by law, because this action will, in their opinion, leave law-abiding citizens at the mercy of gun-owning criminals. Many also believe that gun-control laws will eventually lead to the government taking away all privately owned guns.

Both sides argue their cases passionately. The debate has its roots in colonial history, the fight for independence from Great Britain, and the founding of the United States.

2

Guns and U.S. History

Since arriving in the early seventeenth century, the Europeans who settled in North America used guns to hunt for food. Until the early eighteenth century, they used heavy muskets that had been made in Europe. Starting around 1720, Pennsylvania gunsmiths began making long rifles that fired greater distances and were much more accurate.

In the 1770s, conflict grew between the North American colonists and their British rulers in Great Britain. Fearing an uprising, the British began seizing weapons from the colonists. These

The 1775 Battle of Lexington, fought between the British regular army and militias raised from among ordinary colonial citizens, touched off the Revolutionary War that led to the independence of the American colonies.

seizures brought about violent confrontations between the colonists and the British soldiers. Virginia and other colonies began forming citizen militias, which armed themselves with muskets.

All able-bodied men of a certain age belonged to each colony's militia. Such militias, in the opinion of colonial leaders, would check the power of regular armies, such as the British army. Many colonists saw the British army as wrongly occupying their land and homes. They saw themselves as British citizens being unfairly threatened by the king and his armies.

George Mason and George Washington formed

one of these colonial militias in Fairfax County, Virginia. This militia required each volunteer to keep one firearm, six pounds of gun powder, and twenty pounds of lead (for making bullets) at the ready.[1] Later, Washington would command the Continental Army, a volunteer force whose members came from several different colonies. The long rifles used by Washington's army and the militias played a decisive role in the defeat of British troops during the Revolutionary War.

After independence from Great Britain, James Madison wrote the Second Amendment to the U.S. Constitution. The Congress approved the amendment on September 25, 1789, and then sent it to each state for its approval. By 1791, the Second Amendment was adopted. Guns became an important symbol of the liberties wrested from the British through the skill and courage of the colonists.

During the Revolutionary War, a national armory was established in Springfield, Massachusetts. After independence, the Springfield Armory served as a center for a gun-manufacturing industry in the Connecticut Valley, also known as Gun Valley. Here, important innovations in gun design took place in the early nineteenth century. From Gun Valley, new weapons spread throughout the United States and to its distant frontiers.

Guns on the Frontier and in the City

In Texas of the 1830s and 1840s, frontier Americans fought and won independence from

Mexico with the help of long guns. Soon afterward, on the Great Plains, repeating rifles such as the Springfield, Remington, and Winchester came into use. The Plains settlers hunted game and fought Indians with these repeating rifles and with the .45-caliber revolver, also known as the Peacemaker, invented by Samuel Colt.

The Peacemaker had a revolving chamber that held six bullets. The chamber allowed the owner to fire the gun six times before reloading. The gun first made its mark on the Texas frontier, where a militia

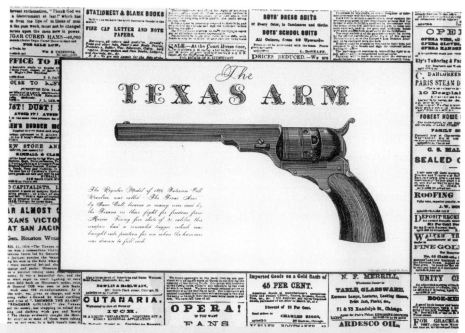

The first revolver, this 1836 Colt revolver manufactured in Paterson, New Jersey, was also known as "The Texas Arm." The weapon could fire five consecutive shots. Its first widespread use was on the unsettled plains of Texas.

known as the Texas Rangers fought hostile Comanche and Apache Indians as well as Mexicans who also claimed the territory. The Indians had the Texans and their single-shot rifles at a disadvantage before the Peacemaker arrived:

> They [Texans] began getting their hands on some of these weapons around 1839, when a few of the revolvers that Sam Colt had built in Paterson [New Jersey] found their way—by means that have never been explained—into the Rangers' camp. By whatever means the guns had arrived there, they were a godsend. During one of the first battles in which the Rangers rode with Colt handguns they killed more than half of an eighty-man Comanche force and put the rest to flight. Colt's gun had shifted the odds decisively in favor of the Texas settlers.[2]

In the meantime, Eastern factories turned out long guns and handguns for a busy market. The leading gun companies included Remington Arms, Winchester, and Smith & Wesson. Under the direction of Sam Colt, a skilled promoter and astute businessman, Colt Firearms became the nation's best-known gunmaker:

> . . . he [Colt] was relentless in his drive to lower prices and thus scare off or bankrupt potential competitors. He used commission sales agents, lobbyists, consignments, and quantity discounts skillfully and . . . was not averse to bribery and blackmail to accomplish his goals. Finally, and to the enduring affection of firearms collectors then and now, Colt used art to bolster the prestige and

At the outbreak of the Civil War in the spring of 1861, members of the 7th New York State Militia take a break at Camp Cameron, District of Columbia. On the Union side, the Civil War was fought by state militias such as these, as well as by the U.S. Army.

soften the associations of a product that was, after all, designed to kill people.[3]

The companies of Gun Valley served a large and expanding market for firearms. On the western frontier, repeating rifles and revolvers became everyday household objects, as common as brooms and coffee pots. In large cities such as San Francisco and New Orleans, citizens also carried firearms, especially the small and easily concealed pistols known as derringers, for self-protection.

Frontier Myths and Gangland Realities

In the 1890s, the United States Army subdued the last American Indians opposing the settlement of the Great Plains. The western frontier of North America closed, and soon a new mythology of the Old West took hold. Books, magazines, and motion pictures celebrated the heroics of frontier settlers and

The .45 caliber Colt revolver found wide acceptance among the cowboys, lawmen, and outlaws of the western frontier. The revolver allowed its owners to fire six shots without reloading, a crucial advantage over muskets and rifles, which had to be reloaded after each shot.

This 1913 Saturday Evening Post *advertisement targets
women consumers in search of reliable means of self-defense.
The idea was to make women believe it was easy to shoot
a gun.*

cowboys. Guns played a central role in these legends and in the stories of famous Western outlaws such as Billy the Kid and Jesse James.

Guns remained a part of everyday life, especially among people living in rural areas. But in the cities, where hunting and target shooting were less common, the public began associating guns with criminals. After World War I, the federal government passed, and the states ratified (by January 1919), the Eighteenth Amendment. The amendment banned the manufacture, transport, and sale of alcohol. During the era of national Prohibition, which officially began in 1920, criminal gangs serving the vast market for liquor armed themselves with handguns, shotguns, and machine guns.

Chicago, in particular, got a bad reputation as a violent gangland haven. On St. Valentine's Day, 1929, members of the Al Capone gang massacred seven of their rivals with machine guns in a Chicago garage. The murders shocked the nation. Citizens and lawmakers demanded more

Al Capone was a leading gangster in the Prohibition years. He and his gangs committed many of their crimes with machine guns.

In the 1929 St. Valentine's Day Massacre, seven gangsters were murdered in a Chicago garage. A frightening tide of crime and gangsterism in the cities was bringing a national outcry for some form of gun control, which would be answered by the National Firearms Act of 1934.

severe punishment for gangsters. They also began to demand some legal controls on deadly weapons.

Prohibition ended in 1933, during a worldwide economic collapse known as the Great Depression. Spectacular crimes took place during the Depression. Bandits and bank robbers such as John Dillinger, "Machine Gun" Kelly, and Bonnie and Clyde inspired big newspaper headlines. Books and movies were made about these crimes. Actors such as Edward G. Robinson, Jimmy Cagney, and George Raft portrayed well-armed killers in popular gangster films. In reaction to the crime wave, the federal government passed the first federal gun-control law in 1934. Another such law was passed in 1938.

The United States fought in World War II from 1941 until 1945. After the war, the nation enjoyed a long period of peace. The Depression and Prohibition eras were forgotten. But in the 1960s, a new crime wave hit the cities of the United States. At the same time, inexpensive handguns became readily available to peaceful citizens as well as criminals. The price of handguns, most assembled from imported parts, fell to less than one hundred dollars. These "Saturday Night Specials" first earned their nickname in Detroit, where many residents bought cheap handguns on the weekends, when crime and violence rates were high.

Between 1963 and 1973, 46,121 U.S. citizens were killed while fighting in the Vietnam War. During the same period, 84,644 civilians were murdered by guns within the United States.[4] About half of all of these murders were committed with handguns.

The Reason for Crime

Why did the United States suffer a crime wave during the 1960s? Many American cities had high levels of poverty and unemployment. Members of the middle class moved to the suburbs, leaving behind poor city neighborhoods. The flight to the suburbs transformed urban neighborhoods into ghettos, where poverty and joblessness fed growing anger and crime. Debates over racial integration, civil rights, school busing, and the Vietnam War bitterly divided the generations and economic classes.

A rising number of voters supported tough gun-control laws as one possible solution to the crime problem. But everybody did not agree that economic conditions and the easy availability of handguns were to blame for the rising crime rate. Instead, many blamed modern culture and the breakdown of traditional morality. There seemed to be no respect among younger people for their parents' generation. Families were changing. Divorce became more common, and many children grew up with a single parent. To find the reason for crime, some people pointed to statistics showing that young males, especially teenagers from broken homes, were committing most violent acts.

Many elected lawmakers called for stricter laws on guns. But gun-control opponents spoke out loudly in defense of gun ownership. They did not want more laws controlling guns. Firearms were not responsible for crimes, in their opinion. Rather, individuals misusing firearms were responsible for crimes. Instead of gun control, the United States needed tougher enforcement of the laws already on the books. The criminal justice system treated thieves, murderers, and hijackers too easily, gun-control opponents maintained.

Opponents of gun control also feared that passage of any gun-control measure would eventually lead to repeal of the Second Amendment. This would end with the banning of all guns, whether they were used for hunting, sport shooting, target practice, or self-defense. If guns were outlawed, these opponents promised, only outlaws would have guns—and law-abiding citizens would be helpless to fight armed criminals.

In 1975, Harlon Carter, a prominent leader of the National Rifle Association, testified to the U.S. Congress on a proposed fourteen-day waiting period for the purchase of handguns:

> It is kind of like the old Bert Lahr commercial that used to be on television. He used to eat a potato chip and say "I'll bet you can't eat just one." And I have no doubt at all that if it is a good thing to be in favor of a fourteen-day waiting period [for the purchase of a handgun], next year [the federal government] is going to be back and say we cannot do it in fourteen days. We will have to take ninety. Frankly, I can see where that leads, knowing how bureaucracies work. It is a little nibble first, and I'll bet you can't eat just one.[5]

By this time, Carter had become a leading opponent of gun-control laws. Carter knew firsthand the value of firearms in self-defense. While growing up near the Texas–Mexico border, he had used a shotgun to kill a young Mexican American. He thought the victim had been threatening his family. Carter was convicted of murder, but his conviction was overturned on appeal.

Cheap handguns were used in the attempt to assassinate President Ronald Reagan in 1981, in the shooting of Alabama Governor George Wallace, and in the murder of John Lennon, a member of the Beatles rock group. During the attempt on Reagan's life, the president's press secretary, James Brady, was shot in the head and permanently disabled. Brady and his wife, Sarah Brady, would soon begin helping the movement for stricter control of handguns.

The attacks and the assassinations did not lessen the public taste for violent entertainment. As in the 1930s and earlier, fictional crime remained a main ingredient of motion pictures. Television producers also relied on violence, using flashy guns as props. Many observers claimed that the 1980s television police show *Miami Vice* did much to boost the sale of "assault weapons" (guns specially manufactured or modified to boost their power, accuracy, and capacity). Many of the criminals on *Miami Vice* used assault weapons that soon afterward were used by real-life drug traffickers and gangsters.

After *Miami Vice* ended its television run, assault weapons became the focus of the gun-control debate. Many believed that violence in entertainment brought about violence in the real world. Author Erik Larson comments,

> Our movies and TV shows do far more damage than simply boosting the appeal of weapons, however. They teach a uniquely American lesson: when a real man has a problem, he gets his gun. He slaps in a clip [of ammunition], he squints grimly into the hot noon sun, then does what he's gotta do.[6]

The Many Gun Laws

Both sides of the gun debate admit firearms laws in the United States are much more lax than in most other countries. The United States does not have a nationwide system of gun licensing, in which gun owners apply for permits to buy and own weapons. Nor does the federal government register guns (keep a record of their sale and ownership). Federal law does require gun purchasers to fill out a form and identify themselves as residents of the state where they make the purchase. It requires background checks to make sure gun buyers are not convicted felons, mentally ill, or under a restraining order (which prevents them from having contact with people thought to be in danger from them). In addition, federal law has banned nineteen different types of semiautomatic assault weapons (these same weapons remain legal if they were bought before September 13, 1994).

The United States also has a big patchwork of local and state gun laws. Typically, the legal possession of firearms is much easier in rural areas than in cities, as many large cities have tough laws against the purchase and possession of weapons. It is generally easier to buy a gun in the West and the South than in the Northeast. In his article "Andy Get Your Gun," writer Andrew Stuttaford described trying to buy a gun in New York:

> New York City's [gun] licensing system has turned a right into a privilege. Like all privileges, it's enjoyed only by the few. There may be more than 7 million people in the five [city] boroughs, but only 40,000 people have valid handgun permits. . . . There aren't many gun-license applications each year (between

one and two thousand), but when it comes to processing them, the city that never sleeps, dozes off. The applicant just has to wait, hoping that his home can be a castle even without a cannon.[7]

Individuals wishing to overcome local laws can either travel to another state, buy their weapons at a gun show where laws are easier, or buy from another private individual. Private citizens are not required by federal law to fill out any forms, conduct background checks, or set a waiting period when selling a gun.

Living With Guns

For many people in the United States, guns are familiar objects. They make up a part of the household, like a color television set or a humming refrigerator in the kitchen. Guns can also be extremely useful. They can be used for target practice, for hunting, or for ridding one's land of unwanted wild animals, such as raccoons, gophers, foxes, and wolves.

For many people, guns also represent something more important. They stand for a better time in the past, when skilled hunters had to depend on their weapons and their wits to put food on the family's table. Guns represent the freedom of the cowboy and the excitement of the Wild West, times more interesting and adventurous than the bland, safe modern world. As young boys, American males looked up to gun-toting heroes in movies and on television. They learned to shoot with BB guns and .22 caliber rifles. They spent endless afternoons in backyards and playgrounds with plastic six-shooters and cap guns.

As young women, American females have different role models—but they also feel a stronger need to defend themselves against criminals.

Neither side—pro-gun or anti-gun—downplays the statistics of gun violence. In 1998, there were 30,708 firearms deaths in the United States. There were 17,424 suicides, 12,102 murders, 866 accidents, and 316 deaths that may have been either accidents or suicides.[8]

Those on opposite sides of the gun debate agree the nation has a problem, but they blame the problem on very different causes. During the past thirty years, they have found little common ground on which to agree. Arising during the bitter social conflicts of the 1960s, the modern gun-control debate remains one of the country's most difficult and long-lasting controversies.

3

The Law

Basically, the gun-control controversy is a debate over law and the role of government. One's view of gun control often depends on one's view of government. If laws passed by elected officials can improve social conditions, then the United States should pass more laws restricting firearms. But if government should have a limited role, and allow society to work out its own problems, then gun-control measures are useless and harmful. Worse, they threaten individual liberty.

The debate over gun control is about

one hundred years old, dating back to the twentieth century. At this time, the United States was going through important changes. The nation was becoming an urban society, a place where city-dwellers outnumbered the rural population. Millions of immigrants were arriving in search of new economic opportunity. The cities themselves were becoming more crowded, and the rates of violent crime were rising.

Fearing this new wave of crime, New York residents clamored for some kind of control over weapons. The city responded with the Sullivan Law of 1911. The law required all city residents to obtain a police permit for any and all handguns in their possession. The permits were hard to get, especially for the poor and for immigrants. The police issued most handgun permits to the wealthy and to those whose jobs—such as security guard or private detective— might require them to be armed. Although it was meant to lessen crime, the Sullivan Law did not rid New York City of weapons. Guns continued to arrive, illegally, from beyond the city limits. Nor did the Sullivan Law end violence in the city.

Federal firearm laws date back to 1919, when the War Revenue Act created the first tax on manufacturers of firearms and ammunition. This law directed that the new tax revenues would pay for the arms and ammunition used to fight World War I. The urban crime wave of the 1920s brought calls for stricter control of pistols, the weapon used in most bank robberies and in gangster-related crime. Many new state and city laws were based on the Uniform

Firearms Act (UFA), passed by the National Conference of Commissioners on Uniform State Laws in 1926.[1] The UFA was a "model" law, one written as an example for states and cities. It required all pistol dealers to be licensed, prohibited convicted criminals from carying pistols, and licensed the carrying of concealed pistols. The UFA also set down a 48-hour "waiting period" before a purchased pistol could be delivered to the buyer. The commissioners thought the waiting-period law would stop crimes committed in the heat of an argument. In theory, those intending murder—and not already owning a gun—might change their minds if forced to wait two days before buying their weapon and committing the deed.

This National Firearms Act, a federal law, passed in 1934. The Act represented a response to the rising tide of Depression-era crime and to an attempted assassination of President Franklin Roosevelt.

John Dillinger, one of the most famous Depression-era gangsters. The public still associated automatic weapons, such as machine guns, with criminals such as Dillinger. As a result the ban on such weapons was widely supported.

The Act restricted and taxed the sale and possession of machine guns, "sawed-off" rifles and shotguns (in which barrels are shortened to allow better concealment), and other common gangster tools such as silencers (which muffle the sound of gunshots). The restricted weapons had to be registered, and their sale was taxed at the rate of two hundred dollars each. Buyers had to submit a photograph, allow themselves to be fingerprinted, and submit to a background check by the Federal Bureau of Investigation (FBI).

John C. Garand aims a .30 caliber M-1 semiautomatic rifle, which he invented. The rifle became standard issue for infantry soldiers in the U.S. Army during World War II.

The National Firearms Act made the Alcohol Tax Unit of the Internal Revenue Service (IRS) responsible for enforcement of the law. Since the passage of this law, not a single weapon of the 175,000 registered under the National Firearms Act has been used to commit a crime.[2]

Later gun laws targeted the dealers who sold firearms to the public. The Federal Firearms Act of 1938 made it illegal to sell firearms across state lines. Selling firearms to convicted felons and fugitives also became a crime. Before doing business, all gun dealers, manufacturers, and importers had to register with the Treasury Department and apply for a federal license, which cost one dollar. The fee was set this low in order to make complying with the law as easy as possible.

The Gun Control Act

On November 22, 1963, President John F. Kennedy was assassinated in Dallas, Texas. The assassin, Lee Harvey Oswald, used an inexpensive Mannlicher-Carcano rifle that he had ordered through the mail. Oswald had seen the rifle advertised in the pages of *American Rifleman*, the official journal of the National Rifle Association. A few days after the assassination, Oswald himself was killed with a concealed handgun wielded by a Dallas nightclub owner named Jack Ruby. In 1968, Senator Robert F. Kennedy, President Kennedy's brother, was assassinated in Los Angeles while campaigning for the presidency. In the same year, civil rights leader

Jack Ruby shoots Lee Harvey Oswald in a Dallas police station, as police and journalists look on. The killing of President Kennedy and Oswald in November 1963 caused a new outcry for gun control, and led to the banning of mail-order rifles such as the weapon Oswald had used to assassinate the president.

Martin Luther King, Jr., was shot down in Memphis. These events again focused the public and its elected representatives on the gun-control debate.

The explosion of urban crime and violence in the 1960s brought new demands for the control of firearms. The result was the Gun Control Act (GCA) of 1968, the most sweeping gun-control legislation yet. The GCA banned cheap Saturday Night Specials by setting minimum size and performance requirements for handguns. But the law only targeted foreign importers—it did not set the same standards for domestic gunmakers. As a result, gunmaking companies went around the GCA's restrictions by importing gun parts and assembling them into complete guns in the United States. Foreign companies also established branches in the United States to go around the law.

The GCA raised the license fee (to ten dollars) for gun dealers, who had to start keeping detailed records of all guns they bought and sold. The law banned the sale of handguns to minors and the sale of rifles, shotguns, and handguns to convicted felons as well as known drug addicts and others thought unfit to own weapons. In response to the assassination of President Kennedy, the GCA also prohibited the sale of guns to individuals through the mail.

The GCA set off a strong protest among those opposing further gun-control legislation. With the election of President Ronald Reagan in 1980, this side of the debate gained a staunch ally in the White House. In 1986, the Congress passed and President Reagan signed the Firearms Owners' Protection Act. The authors of this law intended to "fine-tune" the Gun Control Act to make it friendlier to gun owners and sellers. Among many other things, the 1986 law allowed the interstate sale of long guns (rifles and shotguns). It also eased the penalties on gun dealers found to be violating the GCA.

The Brady Bill

The next major gun-control legislation was named for James Brady, the press secretary severely wounded during the attempt to assassinate President Reagan in 1981. The Brady Handgun Violence Protection Act (Brady Bill), which was passed and signed into law in 1993, imposed a national five-day waiting period for a gun purchase. The law required "instant" background checks on gun purchasers to begin in November 1998, when a national computerized database would be set up. The Brady Bill also increased license fees for gun dealers.

Background checks by the FBI and local police departments actually began in 1994. Through 1999, 22.3 million applications for gun purchases were made, and 536,000 were rejected, a rejection rate of 2.4 percent.[3] The law states that a person with a felony conviction, with a mental illness, or a record of domestic violence may not buy a gun.

Soon after the passage of the Brady Bill, another gun-control bill was proposed. It is known as the Gun Violence Prevention Act of 1994 (or Brady II). This law has not yet been passed. Among other things, Brady II would require a license and fingerprinting to buy a handgun, would set up national registration of gun transfers, would require a special license to own more than one thousand rounds of ammunition, and would limit gun sales to one per month for any individual. It would also ban more varieties of semiautomatic assault weapons and allow lawsuits against gun manufacturers and sellers.

Gun-control opponents and supporters recognize this proposed law as the most restrictive yet on the sale and ownership of firearms. The NRA, one of the most powerful public associations in the country, vows to stop Brady II. Gun-control opponents claim that national registration can lead to confiscation of all firearms by the federal government. Those favoring gun control see Brady II as a reasonable response to the tide of murderous rampages and the possession of dangerous weapons by minors.

The Problem With Laws

There are thousands of federal, state, and local statutes controlling the use, sale, and possession of firearms in the United States. Gun-control opponents point to this fact to support their argument that further laws are unnecessary. If gun laws deter gun violence, they point out, then they should do so in those cities and states where they have passed. But in areas with the strictest laws, such as Washington, D.C., the crime and murder rates remain high. Therefore such laws are ineffective, gun-control opponents say.

Gun-control proponents answer that the patchwork nature of gun laws, which vary from state to state and city to city, makes them ineffective. Proponents also believe there are too many laws. Instead of thousands of local laws, there should be uniform laws that are in force throughout the country. Author Erik Larson, in his book *Lethal Passage*, makes this point: ". . . gaps in existing federal laws, and the utter lack of uniform regulations governing most other aspects of fire-arms transactions, create insane juxtapositions of regulation and deregulation at those points where federal and state laws intersect."[4]

The Sullivan Law, enforced only in New York City, did nothing to stop gun purchases outside the city. Nor did the Sullivan Law toughen the penalties against people committing crimes with handguns. Washington, D.C., continued to experience high crime rates, despite its ban on handgun sales, while the state of Virginia, with its looser laws, became an important source of guns for Washington's criminals. (In response to this phenomenon, Virginia passed a "One Gun Per Month" law in February 1993. Guns then began arriving in Washington from other eastern states.)

To gun-control supporters, gun laws should be passed at the federal level and enforced uniformly all over the country. This would make it easier for the police to understand and enforce the laws and to track down and arrest criminals. National registration of guns would also prevent guns from getting into the wrong hands, supporters believe. It would help cities where tough gun laws do not prevent weapons from passing the city limits

Gun-control opponents see federal laws, and federal agencies that must enforce them, as unfair to local governments, which know best how to deal with local problems such as illegal weapons and street crime. They also fear that federal laws will bring about a stricter control over the behavior and actions of individual citizens. More federal laws, in other words, may bring about the tyranny that the American colonists fought against in the eighteenth century.

Better Weapons, More Laws

The improved firearms of the twentieth century became another focus of the gun-control debate. This controversy dates back to the Prohibition era. During Prohibition, one of the best-known and most destructive weapons was the Thompson submachine gun. The "tommy gun" was a fully automatic weapon, designed for the military but used by many criminal gangs. It could fire hundreds of rounds with a single pull of the trigger. It was heavy and difficult to use, but the deadly hail of bullets from the tommy gun became a hallmark of gangster imagery in movies, cartoons, and books. In 1934, the National Firearms Act restricted the sale of such automatic weapons. Anyone wishing to buy a fully automatic weapon must obtain a license, pass a fingerprint and background check, get a letter of permission from the local police department, pay very high fees, and wait six months.

The 1930s debate over automatic weapons was brief. Most people, including the NRA and its members, favored restrictions on these weapons. Then, beginning in the 1960s, the modern controversy over semiautomatic and assault weapons erupted.

At this time, gun manufacturers were making important changes in the design of certain firearms.

Hoping to cut their costs, they replaced wood with plastic for the stocks (or handles) of their weapons. They shortened the barrels of long guns and replaced their traditional stocks with pistol grips. Magazines, which store ammunition within the weapon, expanded to hold as many as one hundred rounds.

Assault weapons were also designed to fire small-caliber ammunition, which lessens the awkward, upward movement of a gun while it is being fired rapidly. Gun manufacturers also placed metal shrouds over the gun barrels (the shrouds make it easier for the user to hold and aim the hot barrel after the weapon has begun firing). The new weapons were also semiautomatic, meaning that the firearm automatically reloads after each round is fired. With a small and easy modification, carried out by the dealer or the owner, many of the same weapons could be changed to fully automatic machine guns.

The Trouble With Assault Weapons

The new features created a new category of weapon: assault weapons. The Uzi submachine gun, made in Israel, and the AK-47 rifle are among the best known assault weapons. Such firearms originally were designed for military use, in which a trained soldier uses them to fire as many rounds as quickly as possible at a small area or target. Eventually, a large civilian market for assault weapons developed in the United States. By the 1980s, gun manufacturers around the world were selling assault weapons to United States civilians.

Once again, a tragic incident catalyzed public opinion and led to a bruising fight over new federal laws and restrictions. On January 17, 1989, Patrick Purdy brought a modified AK-47 semiautomatic rifle to the edge of a school playground in Stockton, California. Purdy, a mentally ill individual with a paranoid hatred of foreigners, targeted the sons and daughters of southeast Asians who had immigrated to the city of Stockton after the Vietnam War. He opened fire on the schoolyard, killing five Asian-American children, wounded twenty-nine other children and a teacher, and then shot himself dead.

The Stockton attack brought a long and loud public outcry over the sale of assault rifles. In news reports and in the public mind, Purdy's weapon, the AK–47, came to represent the danger of an entire class of weapons. Originally this weapon was manufactured in the Soviet Union for the Soviet military. Soviet troops could use it as a fully automatic or as a semiautomatic weapon. Communist China also manufactured AK–47s, which became the principal weapon of North Vietnamese and Viet Cong troops fighting the United States during the Vietnam War. In 1987, China began exporting thousands of cheap semiautomatic AK–47s to the United States.

On February 6, 1989, just three weeks after the schoolyard shootings, Stockton passed a total ban on assault weapons. California banned forty different types of assault weapons in March. In the same year, Denver, Colorado, banned ownership or sale of assault weapons. Many other cities, including

Cleveland, Los Angeles, Atlanta, and Albany have banned all assault weapons within their city limits.

At this time, the administration of President George Bush supported a ban on the import of assault weapons. But the NRA and other pro-gun groups opposed these and other local laws against assault weapons. They said that the type of weapon—whether a handgun, a rifle, or a semiautomatic rifle—was not the issue. The issue, rather, was a criminal justice system that does not punish criminals. Assault weapons were not used in that many crimes, anyway, said gun-control advocates. Instead, in their opinion, politicians were using the issue for publicity and to get votes at election time.

Gun-control supporters pointed out that assault weapons had no practical purpose other than in criminal use. They were being used not for hunting, but for mass homicides. An effective way to fight crime, in their opinion, would be to take these tools of the criminal out of circulation—by banning them by law, making their possession punishable by fines and jail terms, and confiscating them wherever they might be found.

President Bill Clinton signed the Violent Crime Control and Law Enforcement Act of 1994. The law banned the manufacture, sale, and possession of nineteen different kinds of semiautomatic assault rifles, including the Uzi and the AK-47. This bill also limited the capacity of gun magazines to no more than ten rounds of ammunition. The law allowed gun owners to keep any and all weapons they had purchased before the law went into effect, whether such weapons were now illegal or not.

The assault-weapons ban was one of many features of the 1994 law. The law also authorized new federal spending for crime prevention programs. But the ban became the best known and most bitterly debated section of the law because the opposing groups concerned with gun control made the assault-weapons ban the focus of their argument. The most prominent group favoring gun control was Handgun Control, Inc., while the National Rifle Association remained the most powerful group opposing gun control. By this time, the gun-control debate had come to include issues surrounding these two groups, their ideals, and their tactics. Many people in the United States have strong feelings about gun control, but these groups have been the most prominent advocates of the pro and con sides.

4

The NRA and Gun Control

During the 1990s, the rate of robbery, murder, and other serious crimes fell throughout the United States. The streets of big cities such as New York, Chicago, and Los Angeles grew safer. But in the late 1990s, even as the crime rate declined, violent rampages and school shootings took place. The debate over gun control continued, and in many ways grew more bitter.

Among the general public, the National Rifle Association (NRA) symbolized opposition to gun control. This organization was founded in 1871 in New

The founders of the NRA wanted to improve the shooting skills of the men in the public militias. In America, the militia or citizen soldiers took part in the Battle of Concord in 1775, shown here.

York. It later moved its headquarters to Washington, D.C. Originally, the NRA served as an association for instructing and rewarding rifle marksmanship. Its founders sought to improve the shooting skill of public militias (by the late nineteenth century, "militia" meant state National Guard units). Through the early decades of the twentieth century, the NRA represented hunters, part-time soldiers, and sport rifle shooters. It had little to do with politics or lawmaking.

Nevertheless, the National Rifle Association has long said that gun-control laws are harmful to public safety and liberty. It has opposed such laws since at least 1934, when the U.S. Congress proposed the National Firearms Act. As originally written, the law would have strictly controlled the sale of sawed-off rifles and shotguns and automatic machine guns. It would also have required registration of all handguns in the United States.

The leaders of the NRA agreed that sawed-off guns and machine guns should be controlled. The public, and recreational gun users, associated these weapons only with criminals. But the NRA opposed handgun registration. To fight it, the group sent out editorials and press releases to the media. It also sent letters to its members, asking them to send letters and telegrams to their representatives. There was no similar private association fighting for gun registration. As a result, Congress agreed to change the law to the NRA's satisfaction before passing it.

The Cincinnati Revolt

Over the next thirty years, the NRA remained a sporting association. It was made up of gun enthusiasts, hunters, target shooters, and gun collectors. NRA membership grew steadily after World War II, when many returning veterans took up recreational shooting. The NRA's monthly journal, *American Rifleman*, carried articles and advertisements about guns, ammunition, hunting, and U.S. history.

Then Congress passed the Gun Control Act of 1968. This sweeping new law split the NRA into two factions. General Franklin Orth, then executive vice president of the organization, publicly supported the

Gun Control Act. Those against it rallied around Harlon Carter, a hard-line opponent of gun control. The rivalry continued until 1977, when the NRA held its annual convention in Cincinnati. The NRA members at the convention elected Carter as the new executive vice president. This position is the most powerful within the NRA. In effect, the executive vice president runs the organization.

The "Cincinnati Revolt" changed the NRA. It had once been a hunting and sports-shooting organization. Now it was something more: a lobbying group that fought against gun-control legislation. Under Carter's leadership, the NRA began supporting candidates for political office. It fought new gun legislation by urging members to join its letter-writing campaigns. It criticized the Bureau of Alcohol, Tobacco, and Firearms (ATF), which is responsible for enforcing federal laws concerning guns.

The leaders of the NRA view gun-control laws as contrary to the Second Amendment of the U.S. Constitution. The NRA also sees private gun ownership as a guarantee of constitutional rights. The NRA fears that the ultimate goal of gun legislation is the confiscation of all guns from private citizens, even those using guns for legal and peaceful activities. To the NRA, the fact that many police agencies support gun control just confirms their fears. Many NRA members see gun laws leading to a time when only the state and its agencies, such as the ATF, the military, the Federal Bureau of Investigation (FBI), and local police officers—as well as criminals—will own guns.

The NRA's current executive vice president,

Wayne LaPierre, summed up these sentiments in his book, *Guns, Crime, and Freedom*. Commenting on a proposed ban on assault weapons in New Jersey, LaPierre wrote, "The thought of law enforcement officials supporting measures to take firearms from law-abiding citizens conjures up images of a police state."[1]

The NRA opposes gun-control laws on national and local levels. The organization strongly opposes state and city laws that can be used as models for similar legislation in other parts of the nation. In 1988, legislators in Maryland proposed an outright ban on the sale and manufacture of cheap handguns, or "Saturday Night Specials." After the ban passed, the NRA organized a petition drive among Maryland residents. The petition asked that a state referendum be held on the new law. In a referendum, the voters have a chance to accept or reject proposed new laws.

The NRA saw this as a crucial fight. Maryland is the home of many federal workers and members of Congress, and 1988 was a presidential election year. The NRA spent nearly $7 million on its efforts.

After enough signatures in favor of the referendum were collected, the NRA began a statewide publicity campaign. Both gun-control opponents and supporters sent out letters, made phone calls, and canvassed neighborhoods. The opponents walked door-to-door to persuade citizens to vote against the ban. But on election day, the ban was upheld by a margin of 52 to 48 percent.

The NRA supports legislation that weakens restrictions on guns. In May 1986, the U.S.

Congress passed the Firearms Owners' Protection
Act (also known as the McClure-Volkmer Act). This
law banned the manufacture, sale, and possession
of unregistered machine guns. But it also ended a
requirement for gun dealers to record ammunition
sales. This act allowed the sales of rifles and shotguns
across state lines. It barred the federal government
from creating a central registry (file) of dealer records.
The NRA strongly opposes such recordkeeping by the
U.S. government. Its leaders and members fear that
the real purpose of registration is to keep an eye on
law-abiding, gun-owning citizens and make it easier
to confiscate registered guns.

The NRA uses many effective weapons in the
fight against gun control. One of the most common is
the Legislative Alert. The Legislative Alert goes into
action whenever a new gun-control measure is intro-
duced. A letter is sent to every NRA member, asking
that the member write or call his or her representative in Congress and demand that the new law be
opposed. A Legislative Alert includes an appeal for
donations to help the organization pay for its mail-
ings and other activities.

"Cop-Killer" Bullets

Many gun-control supporters favor restrictions on
ammunition as well as guns. But the NRA strongly
opposes new laws on ammunition. It also opposes
any restrictions on new firearms technology. The
NRA believes that ordinary people should not be

legally deprived of tools that also can be acquired by criminals.

In the early 1980s, a debate broke out over the manufacture and sale of armor-piercing bullets. These bullets were invented in the 1970s by Dr. Paul Kopsch, Daniel Turcus, and Donald Ward. Originally, the three men hoped their invention would help the police. They wanted to create a bullet that would allow police officers to fire through car doors (in many shoot-outs, criminals hide behind car doors).

On impact, ordinary lead bullets spread out and deform, an effect that stops them from penetrating heavy metal objects. But the new "KTW" bullets (named after the three men who invented them) are coated with Teflon, a substance that lessens the spreading effect and allowed the bullets to easily penetrate metal. Unfortunately, the bullets also can easily penetrate the bulletproof vests commonly used by the police. The KTW bullets also ricochet dangerously after firing. This puts by-standers and other police officers in as much danger as their criminal targets.

For these reasons, the KTW bullet was not adopted by most police departments. Those departments that did adopt the bullet eventually dropped it. Yet in the early 1980s, licensed firearms dealers were still selling KTW bullets to the public. Many people learned this by watching a national news program aired by the NBC television network. The report caused a sensation, bringing a loud public outcry—in the form of letters to legislators and newspaper editorials—against "cop-killer" bullets.

Soon afterward, the members of a New York police union asked their congressman, Mario Biaggi, to write a law banning the bullets. A former police officer himself, Biaggi agreed.

Despite its traditional association with the police and law enforcement, the NRA fought Biaggi's legislation. If KTW bullets could be banned because they posed a danger to police officers, then so, eventually, could certain kinds of concealed handguns. In addition, Biaggi's law banned other kinds of ammunition used by hunters and recreational shooters. The leaders of the NRA believed that newspapers and television shows were sensationalizing the issue. They saw a danger of the United States sliding down a slippery slope of new laws and restrictions.

The NRA wrote to its members, urging them to call and write their representatives in Congress and urge opposition to the ban. One part of the mailing read:

> . . . The so-called "cop-killer" bullet issue is a Trojan Horse waiting outside gun-owners' doors. If the anti-gunners have their way, this highly publicized and emotionalized issue will be used to enact a backdoor, national gun control scheme. . . The anti-gun forces will go to any lengths to void your right to keep and bear arms. It's time we set them straight! I am asking you—each and every NRA member and your friends—to flood the United States Congress with your letters.[2]

The letter-writing campaign was only the beginning. NRA members appeared at local city council meetings, where council members debated new laws against cop-killer bullets. The members stood and criticized the proposed new laws. They made it loud and clear that their support in the next election depended on the vote on armor-piercing bullets.

But the NRA's opposition to the ban caused outrage among police officers and even angered some NRA members. Those groups supporting gun control, particularly Handgun Control, Inc., saw this as a chance to weaken the NRA's standing among the general public. As Josh Sugarmann, director of a pro-gun control group known as the Violence Policy Center, explains: "Handgun Control, Inc. . . . moved quickly to push cop-killer bullets to the front of its political program. A relationship previously thought impossible could now be built. HCI's message wasn't subtle: The NRA was literally willing to sacrifice cops for the sake of ideological purity. To put it more bluntly—the NRA killed cops."[3]

The two sides bitterly debated the ban on cop-killer bullets. Finally, in 1985, they reached a compromise. At this time, the NRA was fighting for passage of the McClure-Volkmer Act, which banned certain machine guns, but ended a requirement for gun dealers to record ammunition sales. Because NRA leaders wanted the support of police groups for this law, it stopped opposing the ban on armor-piercing ammunition. Named the Law Enforcement Officers' Protection Act of 1986, the law banning KTW and other kinds of armor-piercing bullets passed the U.S. Congress in December 1985. President Reagan signed the law in August 1986.

Plastic Guns

The NRA did not want to anger the nation's police officers. Its leaders knew that police officers, because they deal with crime on a daily basis, made valuable allies for either side of the gun-control debate. The NRA and all other groups in the debate also want to win the support of the majority of United States citizens, and most of these citizens are on the side of the police.

After the KTW bullet issue died down, another gun-control issue quickly arose to take its place. In early 1986, the imported semiautomatic pistol known as the Glock 17 was making headlines. At this time the public's fear of terrorism, especially the bombing and hijacking of airplanes, was running high. Some news reports described the Glock 17 and its plastic frame. According to these reports, the frame allowed the gun to pass through airport security scanners without being detected.

Legislators called for new laws to ban the Glock and other guns that contained a certain percentage of plastic (and other undetectable materials). The NRA opposed the ban. Handgun Control, Inc. and other gun-control supporters favored it. At this time, the administration of President Ronald Reagan was seeking to "mend fences" with police groups, many of whom opposed the McClure-Volkmer bill. Attorney General Edwin Meese helped write a new law on plastic guns. This legislation would ban any and all guns that were difficult to detect by security scanners.

The NRA made an all-out lobbying effort against the law. It argued that a ban on guns defined as "difficult to detect" was too vague. Such a law might be enforced against smaller guns, not just plastic guns. It might then lead to more laws and the outright banning of all guns.

The leaders of the NRA arranged a meeting between Senator James McClure, an important NRA ally in Congress, and Vice President George Bush. During the meeting, McClure persuaded Bush to talk to the attorney general and pressure Meese to withdraw support for the law against plastic guns. Eventually, the lobbying effort succeeded. Attorney General Meese agreed to oppose the law that he had helped to write.

During the 1988 presidential campaign, however, candidate George Bush came out for a ban on undetectable guns. Bush's new stand disappointed the NRA. Senator McClure then offered a new law that would ban handguns with less than 3.7 ounces of steel. This was a compromise law, and not as strict. The original legislation would have banned guns with less than 8.5 ounces of steel. As a result, it would have banned a much wider variety of weapons.

McClure's new law, the Terrorist Firearms Detection Act, passed in Congress and was signed into law by President Reagan on November 11, 1988. The law did not end the use of the Glock 17, which remained a legal weapon. In fact, the Glock is now the standard sidearm used by many big-city police forces.

The Star of the NRA

During the controversies over cop-killer bullets and plastic guns, film star Charlton Heston emerged as a spokesman for the NRA. For millions of filmgoers, he had become a symbolic and sympathetic authority figure through such famous movie roles as Moses in *The Ten Commandments* and as a Roman-era slave and champion charioteer in *Ben-Hur*. He has played American pioneers, saints, soldiers, kings, presidents, and the Renaissance painter Michelangelo.

Heston took his roles and his responsibilities seriously. He also took a strong interest in politics and public affairs. In 1968, he signed a statement to President Lyndon Baines Johnson in support of the Gun Control Act. The statement said in part:

> Our gun control laws are so lax that anyone can buy a weapon . . . 6,300 people are murdered every year with firearms in these United States. This is an outrage and when it is compared with the far, far lower rates in other free countries, it is intolerable. Like most Americans, we share the conviction that stronger gun control legislation is mandatory in this tragic situation.[4]

Later, Heston formed his own political action committee, known as the ARENA PAC, to raise funds for political candidates who agree with his views. By the 1990s, he had changed his mind on gun-control laws, and he closely associated himself with the National Rifle Association. In 1996, he was elected president of the NRA. He was re-elected again in 1998 and in 2000. His familiarity and his popularity make him a valuable spokesman for the

NRA, perhaps the most effective spokesman in the organization's history.

Heston spares no words in his anti-gun-control crusade. In his speeches and media appearances, he portrays the fight over gun control as an epic struggle between the forces of traditional American liberty versus wrongheaded gun-control advocates. For Heston, as for many NRA members, the long rifle of the early settlers and colonial militias symbolizes liberty more than any other object, statute, document, or painting. In a speech to the National Press Club on September 11, 1997, he commented,

> Our ancestors were armed with pride, and bequeathed it to us—I can prove it. If you want to feel the warm breath of freedom upon your neck . . . If you want to touch the proud pulse of liberty that beat in our founding fathers in the purest form, you can do so through the majesty of the Second Amendment right to keep and bear arms.
>
> Because there, in that wooden stock and blued steel, is what gives the most common of common men the most uncommon of freedoms . . . It doesn't matter whether its purpose is to defend our shores or your front door; whether the gun is a rite of passage for a young man or a tool of survival for a young woman; whether it brings meat for the table or trophies for the shelf; without respect to age, or gender, or race, or class, the Second Amendment right to keep and bear arms connects us all—with all that is right—with that sacred document: the Bill of Rights.[5]

By the year 2000, Charlton Heston had become the nation's most familiar gun-control opponent. In fact, he was probably the best known individual in the entire debate. Those against gun control are proud to have him as their advocate. But Heston has also made determined opponents out of people who are equally committed to the other side of the controversy.

5

Gun-control Advocates

In the early 1970s, an armed robber held up a student named Mark Borinsky in a Chicago street. Although he was not hurt, Borinsky had been frightened. After completing his studies, he moved to Washington, D.C. There he founded an organization dedicated to stricter laws and control of handguns. He called this group the National Council to Control Handguns. Later he changed its name to Handgun Control, Inc. (HCI).

Borinsky had no experience in the ways of Washington. He asked for help from Edward Welles, a retired agent of the

Central Intelligence Agency (CIA). He also recruited
N. T. "Pete" Shields, a businessman whose son had
been shot and murdered in San Francisco in 1974.
Welles and Shields both had experience in
Washington. They helped Borinsky turn Handgun
Control into an effective lobbying organization.

Borinsky and his colleagues found that many
legislators, especially Democrats from Eastern states,
supported new gun-control laws. Sympathetic
members of the U.S. Department of Justice also
helped Handgun Control by providing the group with
statistics on guns and gun violence. Police unions
lent their support, and two law firms in Washington,
D.C., offered the pro bono (free) services of their
attorneys and staff.

The leaders of Handgun Control knew that their
opposition—the NRA—was rich and powerful. While
the NRA counted about 3 million members, Handgun
Control began with only a few. While the NRA had
more than a century of organizing and lobbying experience, Handgun Control was new and unknown in
Washington.

Borinsky and his partners decided to take small
steps, one step at a time. They would support minor
gun-control measures, many of them on the local
level, rather than sweeping new federal laws. Soon
after organizing, Handgun Control allied with the
National Coalition to Ban Handguns, a group of
small, nonprofit organizations dedicated to banning
handguns altogether. At first, Handgun Control also
supported this goal. But banning handguns would
mean not only preventing their sale and manufacture

but also taking them away from citizens. There is very little support for such action among the public or lawmakers. So Handgun Control compromised by ending its support for an outright ban. The organization called instead for stricter laws on the sale of handguns. Eventually, it would also seek universal registration of all firearms.

The public's concern over gun violence helped Handgun Control. Every time a spectacular shooting occurred, the group picked up more support. Statistics also gave a boost to the group. Comparing crime rates in the United States with those in Europe and Japan made the United States look bad because of its more lax gun laws. Although it is the wealthiest

Guns purchased illegally in recent decades have been responsible for many of the assassinations and would-be assassinations of famous people, such as John Lennon and Ronald Reagan.

country in the world, the United States is also the nation suffering most from gun violence. As Gregg Lee Carter comments in his book, *The Gun Control Movement*, "The murder of John Lennon in December of 1980—also carried out with a cheap pistol— likewise greatly heightened public and media interest in and sympathy for the kind of strict national control of guns that HCI was promoting. Lennon's assassination took the organization from 5,000 to 80,000 dues-paying members in a matter of weeks."[1]

The Turning Point

The attempt on the life of President Ronald Reagan on March 30, 1981, proved to be a momentous event in the history of Handgun Control. The attack seemed to prove the group's point that handguns were too easily available in the United States. In HCI's view, the simple method of buying a dangerous weapon had almost cost the life of a president.

The previous fall, a young man named John Hinckley had arrived in Dallas, Texas. Hinckley visited a Dallas gun shop and offered as proof of his identity a Texas driver's license. He then filled out a two-page form that all gun buyers must complete when buying firearms from a federally licensed dealer. The form asks the buyer if he or she is a convicted felon, a drug addict, or a foreigner living in the country illegally. It asks if he or she has renounced citizenship in the United States, or been dishonorably discharged from the military.

If any of the questions are answered "Yes," then

the dealer cannot legally sell the gun. If all of the answers are "No," and if the buyer can show that he is a resident of the state, then the purchase can take place. No witnesses to the statements are required. The buyer does not have to prove that he or she is telling the truth. The buyer can simply "lie and buy." The gun dealer keeps the form for his records, in case the police need to examine it later.

In 1980, in the state of Texas, Hinckley did not have to undergo a background check before buying his weapon. Nor did he have a waiting period. He paid twenty-nine dollars for a .22-caliber Rohm RG14 revolver—even though, unknown to the dealer, he had given a false address on the form.

On March 30, 1981, Hinckley arrived outside the Washington Hilton Hill Hotel. He concealed his handgun in the pocket of his coat. In the early afternoon, as President Reagan and his aides left a side door of the hotel, Hinckley opened fire. He was using "Devastator" bullets, designed to explode on impact and cause maximum damage to flesh and bone. Within two seconds, six Devastators sailed into a dense crowd as Hinckley scuffled with Secret Service agents and police officers.

The president was hit in the chest by one bullet that ricocheted off a car. One bullet struck a policeman, Thomas Delahanty, in the back. Another hit Timothy McCarthy, a Secret Service agent. Two of the bullets missed. But the remaining Devastator struck James Brady, Reagan's press secretary, in the forehead. This was the only bullet to

Long Gun Regulations			
State	**Permit**	**Background Check** (time of purchase)	**Waiting Period**
Alabama	none	Federal	none
Alaska	none	Federal	none
Arizona	none	State	none
Arkansas	none	Federal	none
California	none	State	ten days
Colorado	none	State	none
Connecticut	none	State	none
Delaware	none	Federal	none
Florida	none	State	none
Georgia	none	State	none
Hawaii	yes	State	fifteen days[1]
Idaho	none	Federal	none
Illinois	yes	State	one day[2]
Indiana	none	Federal	none
Iowa	none	Federal	none
Kansas	none	Federal	none
Kentucky	none	Federal	none
Louisiana	none	Federal	none
Maine	none	Federal	none
Maryland	none	Federal	none[3]
Massachusetts	yes	Federal	thirty days[1]
Michigan	none	Federal	none[4]
Minnesota	none	Federal	none
Mississippi	none	Federal	none
Missouri	none	Federal	none

1 Waiting period refers to the period it takes to acquire permit.
2 Up to thirty-day waiting period for permit to purchase.
3 Waiting period applies to assault weapon purchases.
4 Waiting period and permit needed for assault weapon purchases.

Long Gun Regulations

State	Permit	Background Check (time of purchase)	Waiting Period
Montana	none	Federal	none
Nebraska	none	Federal	none
Nevada	none	State	none
New Hampshire	none	Federal	none
New Jersey	yes	State	thirty days[1]
New Mexico[5]	none	Federal	none
New York	none	Federal	none
North Carolina	none	Federal	none
North Dakota	none	Federal	none
Ohio	none	Federal	none
Oklahoma	none	Federal	none
Oregon	none	Federal	none
Pennsylvania	none	Federal[6]	none
Rhode Island	none	Federal	none
South Carolina	none	State	none
South Dakota	none	Federal	none
Tennessee	none	State	none
Texas	none	Federal	none
Utah	none	State	none
Vermont	none	State	none
Virginia	none	State	none
Washington	none	Federal	none
West Virginia	none	Federal	none
Wisconsin	none	Federal	none
Wyoming	none	Federal	none

5 New Mexico state background check system may be used in the near future.
6 State background checks on long guns began in December 1999.

work properly and explode. Brady survived, but was permanently and severely disabled.

Just as the assassination of President Kennedy had opened a long debate on gun control, and eventually led to a sweeping new law known as the Gun Control Act of 1968, the attempted assassination of President Reagan also had long-lasting effects. It eventually brought James Brady's wife, Sarah Brady, to Handgun Control, Inc., where she became the organization's most prominent spokesperson.

As a dedicated Republican, Sarah Brady had stood with the party that had strongly opposed gun-control measures. Now her husband had been nearly killed by a cheap handgun. After this event, she found her young son playing with a "toy" gun that turned out to be real. She changed her mind about gun control. In speeches and articles, Brady fought for a seven-day waiting period and a background check for anyone trying to buy a handgun. She made the point that filling out forms did not prevent the wrong people, such as John Hinckley, from getting deadly weapons. Before one congressional subcommittee, she argued that

> . . . We already have a federal law prohibiting convicted felons, minors, people who have been adjudicated mentally ill, illegal aliens, and drug addicts from acquiring handguns. But what does that mean if we do not have the tools to enforce that law? . . . As long as we do not have a reasonable waiting period and give police the opportunity to run background checks, a convicted felon will have our seal of approval . . . Had police

been given an opportunity to discover that Hinckley lied on the federal form, Hinckley might well have been in jail instead of on his way to Washington . . .[2]

During the 1970s, the National Rifle Association had supported such a waiting period. An official statement made by the NRA claimed that "a waiting period could help in reducing crimes of passion and in preventing people with criminal records or dangerous mental illness from acquiring guns."[3] But that was before the Cincinnati Revolt, which changed the NRA's position on waiting periods and other possible new gun-control measures. Under its new leadership, the NRA opposed any and all forms of new gun-control laws, including background checks and waiting periods.

The so-called Brady Bill would not pass under the Reagan administration, nor under that of President George Bush. But it did succeed with the arrival of a Democratic administration that generally supported HCI's methods and goals. Twelve years after the attempted assassination of President Reagan and the wounding of James Brady, the Brady Handgun Violence Prevention Act of 1993 was passed. The revised Brady Bill shortened the national waiting period for handgun purchases from seven to five days. Exceptions are made, however: If the buyer testifies to an immediate need of the weapon for self-protection; if the waiting period is impractical because the buyer lives too far away; or if the buyer has a state permit to own a handgun. In all these cases, the waiting period is dropped.

Handgun Regulations

State	Permit	Background Check (time of purchase)	Waiting Period
Alabama	none	Federal	two days
Alaska	none	Federal	none
Arizona	none	Federal	none
Arkansas	none	Federal	none
California	none	State	ten days
Colorado	none	State	none
Connecticut	yes	State	fourteen days[1]
Delaware	none	Federal	none
Florida	none	State	three day
Georgia	none	State	none
Hawaii	yes	State	fifteen days[1]
Idaho	none	Federal	none
Illinois	yes	State	three days[2]
Indiana	none	State	none
Iowa	yes	State	three days[1]
Kansas	none	Federal	none
Kentucky	none	Federal	none
Louisiana	none	Federal	none
Maine	none	Federal	none
Maryland	none	State	seven days
Massachusetts	yes	Federal	thirty days[1]
Michigan	yes	State	varies[1]
Minnesota	yes	Federal	seven days[1]
Mississippi	none	Federal	none
Missouri	yes	Federal	seven days[1]

1 Waiting period refers to the period it takes to acquire permit.
2 Up to thirty-day waiting period for permit to purchase.
3 New Mexico state background check system may be used in the near future.

Handgun Regulations

State	Permit	Background Check (time of purchase)	Waiting Period
Montana	none	Federal	none
Nebraska	yes	State	two days[1]
Nevada	none	State	none
New Hampshire	none	Federal	none
New Jersey	yes	State	thirty days[1]
New Mexico[3]	none	Federal	none
New York	yes	Federal	six months[1]
North Carolina	yes	State	thirty days[1]
North Dakota	none	Federal	none
Ohio	none	Federal	none
Oklahoma	none	Federal	none
Oregon	none	State	none
Pennsylvania	none	State	none
Rhode Island	none	Federal	seven days
South Carolina	none	State	none
South Dakota	none	Federal	none
Tennessee	none	State	none
Texas	none	Federal	none
Utah	none	State	none
Vermont	none	State	none
Virginia	none	State	none
Washington	none	State	five days
West Virginia	none	Federal	none
Wisconsin	none	State	two days
Wyoming	none	Federal	none

The Brady Bill also mandated an instant criminal background check for all purchasers of handguns. The check was supposed to confirm that buyers were not convicted felons, who by law cannot purchase firearms. For five years, the background check would be carried out by local police forces. On November 30, 1998, the check would be done through a central national database. But in 1997, the U.S. Supreme Court decided that local police forces cannot be required to carry out the background checks. Some states do enforce a longer waiting period as well as background checks using a national criminal information system known as Instacheck.

New Priorities and the Gun Violence Prevention Act

Handgun Control has not been satisfied with the passage of the Brady Bill. It still favors registration of all private sales of handguns. It wants mandatory jail terms for those convicted of unlawful use of firearms and a total ban on Saturday Night Specials. Handgun Control would like gun purchases to be limited to one per month for any buyer. It also believes handgun buyers should go through a program that would train them in the safe use of weapons.

To attain their goals, the leaders of Handgun Control write proposed laws they hope will be passed. They arrange for experts to testify in favor of its goals and lobby for new legislation they want. In answer to the NRA's fears, the group claims that it does not want to take guns out of the hands of law-abiding citizens: "None of the laws HCI supports would deny a law-abiding citizen access to a handgun for any legitimate purpose . . . We are working for passage of a sensible national gun policy, including a federal waiting period for handgun sales, to help screen out criminals, and a ban on the sale and manufacture of non-sporting assault weapons."[4]

To this end, in the mid-1990s, Handgun Control worked with two of its allies in Congress, Senator Howard Metzenbaum of Ohio and Representative Charles Schumer of New York, to write a sweeping new law that makes national gun laws in the United States similar to those of many European countries. The new measures were collected into a new federal law called the Gun Violence Prevention Act, or "Brady II." This law would establish a national handgun license. Among many other things, Brady II would ban the purchase or transfer of more than one handgun at a time. It would also limit handgun purchases to one per month. It would ban all assault weapons and Saturday Night Specials. All firearms would have to be registered with the ATF, and the licensing fee for gun dealers would be raised to one thousand dollars from the ten dollars it has been. It would also establish minimum penalties for violation of firearms laws, possession of firearms by convicted violent felons and drug offenders, and for firearms theft.

By the year 2000, Handgun Control was setting several new gun-control priorities for federal lawmakers. The organization supports "child access prevention," which makes it a crime to leave a gun in reach of a child within the household. The first such law was passed in Florida in 1989, and by 2000 a total of sixteen states had child access laws on their books. HCI also supports one-gun-a-month laws, which limit the number of gun purchases to one per month per buyer. In part, these laws are meant to prevent straw purchases, in which an individual buys several guns for unlicensed dealers who then sell the guns on the street.

HCI wants the federal government to require the sale of trigger locks on each gun, which would, in theory, prevent anyone but the owner from using the gun. Also, HCI is fighting to close the loophole in the 1968 Gun Control Act that allows cheap handguns to be made in the United States. HCI supports laws that would set the same manufacturing and safety standards on American guns as on imported guns.

In late April 2000, after a shooting at the Washington National Zoo, Sarah Brady pointed out the loopholes in local and state laws that still made cities such as Washington, D.C., dangerous places to live in and visit:

> Even the District of Columbia, which has strict gun laws, is prey to the loopholes that allow juveniles and criminals to get guns with ease—at gun shows, over the Internet, at garage sales and flea markets, and in completely unregulated sales between private individuals. . . . We need a universal gunowner licensing system, in which every sale is documented and every gun purchaser checked and photo-licensed. We need to register hand-guns, so that every gun can be immediately traced to its owner. . . . We need

a national one-handgun-a-month law. . . . We need to completely prohibit the possession of handguns by juveniles under age 21, and completely outlaw the large ammunition magazines that make mass shootings so easy . . . if we dismiss this latest public tragedy as something we must accept, we are guaranteeing that future tragedies will occur.[5]

In the summer of 2000, Handgun Control enlisted the support of its own celebrity, Martin Sheen, an actor known for portraying the American president on the television series *West Wing*. In television ads, Sheen appeared before a huge American flag. He criticized the gun-control stand of Texas Governor George W. Bush—who, at the time, was running for president of the United States. Even so, Bush was elected by a narrow margin of electoral votes.

6

Gun Controversies, Old and New

The two sides of the gun-control debate view the issue, and laws surrounding it, from very different perspectives. They have different views of history and of the Second Amendment. They do not always agree on the reason for high crime rates and inner-city violence. Tragic school massacres and cheap Saturday Night Specials divide them into opposing camps. The two sides have also proposed different solutions to the problem of gun violence. When these solutions are put into effect, the two sides interpret the results differently.

Agreeing to Disagree

Gun-control supporters, for example, are strongly in favor of outlawing Saturday Night Specials. They feel that all guns—not just imported guns—should meet certain safety standards. They also believe that because cheaper guns more easily backfire or fire accidentally, they are as dangerous to their owners as they are to criminals.

Some state governments now agree with this idea. Maryland and Massachusetts have banned Saturday Night Specials. All guns sold in Massachusetts must now come with safety warnings. They must carry serial numbers that cannot be changed or filed off. (The serial number makes the gun easier to trace to its first owner.) The guns must also be sold with childproof locks. Semiautomatic guns must have an indicator that shows whether the gun has a bullet in its firing chamber. The indicator is intended to help prevent accidents that occur when people handle loaded guns they mistakenly believe are not loaded.

Gun-control opponents oppose restrictions on cheap handguns. They respond that such a ban will make handguns more expensive, making it more difficult for poor people to buy guns. Many people living in inner cities need guns for protection, they point out, and many such people can afford only inexpensive weapons. As a result, they say, a ban on Saturday Night Specials discriminates against the poor.

Many gun dealers also oppose laws that require childproof locks. These locks make the guns more expensive. In Massachusetts, gun buyers who do not want to buy a gun with a childproof lock can simply drive to New Hampshire, where the locks are not required.

Gun-control supporters also favor gun turn-in programs, at which citizens are urged to give up their weapons voluntarily. In exchange, the owner gets cash (often fifty dollars or one hundred dollars) or a credit on a water or electricity bill. In many cities, public money is used to pay the bounty.

Supporters of such programs believe they help to get weapons off the streets. They also believe gun turn-in programs bring favorable publicity and public awareness of the basic problem: too many guns. When covered on television and in the press, the turn-in programs reveal that hundreds, sometimes thousands, of weapons had been concealed within the community.

Opponents say the buyback programs are "feel-good" programs that help only criminals, who need their weapons for their work and will not turn them in. These programs, in the view of gun-control opponents, also harm innocent citizens who give up an important source of protection in a lawless world.

Those opposing gun-control laws have suggested new measures of their own. One of these is the concealed-carry law, which allows people to apply for a permit to carry a concealed weapon. Gun-control supporters fear that concealed-carry laws only spread more guns around and make the streets more dangerous. Gun-control opponents believe concealed-carry permits help lower crime, as criminals in concealed-carry states can never be sure whether or not their potential victims are armed. The argument favoring concealed carry persuaded many state law-makers, especially in the South—a region with a high rate of gun ownership. Between 1988 and 1994, the NRA helped get concealed-carry laws passed in twenty-eight states. The NRA has also worked with city councils, state governments, and county boards to pass pre-emption laws, which prohibit the city or state from passing any further gun-control measures.

Tougher Laws

Gun-control opponents as well as supporters support tougher laws. One measure has been mandatory sentencing, such as the "three strikes and you're out" rule. With this law, anyone found guilty of three serious crimes must be sentenced to life in prison without parole. The judge who passes sentence has no choice in the matter. California, and several other states, have already passed the three-strikes law. Other new laws set mandatory minimum sentences for those guilty of committing a crime with a gun. In Florida, criminals in possession of guns can get ten years in prison. If they use the gun while committing another crime, they get twenty years. If they shoot somebody during the crime, they get a life sentence.

One of the most successful crime-fighting programs has been Project Exile, which began in Richmond, Virginia. Project Exile sets a five-year jail sentence for any convicted felon caught with a gun. The accused can be jailed no matter what he or she is doing with the gun. Richmond police and community leaders believe Project Exile has helped to reduce serious crime in their city. Since they began the program, other cities have also taken it up.

The Debate and the Amendment

The gun-control debate includes a much deeper argument over the history of the United States. Gun-control opponents celebrate the liberty of colonial-era gunowners. Many of them collect antique muskets and rifles, keeping them as mementos of American history. Some gun-control advocates believe that gun-control opponents have a view of American history that may be more myth than fact. In an interview for the Web site salon.com about his recent book, *Arming America: The Origins of a National Gun Culture*, historian Michael Bellesiles remarked:

> There is no relationship at all between gun ownership in the 18th and 19th centuries and today. And the reason it matters . . . is because the NRA has long associated itself with an imagined history of America in which those who love freedom always owned firearms . . . [the colonial laws] saw guns as belonging to the state. The state had all priority rights over firearms. They could appropriate them at any time without recompense.[1]

The thoughts and ideas of the founders of the United States have been debated for more than two hundred years. So what was James Madison thinking when he wrote the Second Amendment? Madison explained himself as follows in *The Federalist Papers*:

Let a regular army, fully equal to the resources of the country, be formed; and let it be entirely at the devotion of the federal government: still it would not be going too far to say that the State governments with the people on their side would be able to repel the danger . . . a militia amounting to near half a million of citizens with arms in their hands, officered by men chosen from among themselves, fighting for their common liberties and united and conducted by governments possessing their affection and confidence. It may well be doubted whether such a militia . . . could ever be conquered by such a proportion of regular troops. . . . Besides the advantage of being armed, which the Americans possess over the people of almost every other nation, the existence of subordinate [state] governments . . . forms a barrier against the enterprise of ambition. . . .[2]

In other words, Madison saw the amendment as guaranteeing that the people of the United States could effectively fight their own government, if necessary.

Gun-control supporters say that the NRA does not really understand the Second Amendment. In an article in *Legal Times* entitled "Exploding the NRA's Constitutional Myth," written in the spring of 1991 during the debate over the Brady Bill, this point is made:

Whereas the First Amendment addresses freedom of personal belief and expression, the Second Amendment addresses the distribution of military power in society.

Many colonists strongly distrusted a standing army composed of professional soldiers and controlled by the central government. They sought in the Bill of Rights a reaffirmation of the right of the states to have their own armed militia, composed of ordinary citizens, as a check on the power of the standing army.[3]

Originally, the amendment was meant to allow the arming of militias. Since that time, the colonial militias have been transformed into the National Guard, part-time units drawn from civilian volunteers. State governors control National Guard units. They can call out the Guard in times of natural disaster, such as a flood or hurricane, in order to shelter people and stop looting. The Guard also appears during violent demonstrations and riots, when ordinary police forces lose control of the streets. The National Guard is not a civilian militia as James Madison understood them. It does not place a check on a tyrannical government. Instead, it is used by the government to keep order and control unruly crowds.

The tyranny that worried Madison has not come about. The United States holds regular elections, and the representatives are answerable to the voters. The First Amendment guarantees freedom of the press and of public speech. Just in case tyranny does threaten, gun-control opponents want to keep their firearms—as many as they want. Gun-control supporters believe that just as the First Amendment does not give an unlimited power of free speech, the Second does not confer the unlimited right to own firearms of any kind.

At one time, the NRA might have been open to a debate on the Second Amendment. After all, the purpose of the NRA was the training of public militias in rifle marksmanship. In the early twentieth century, the NRA drew on a supply of inexpensive rifles from the United States military—a standing (permanent) army. In the 1930s, the NRA interpreted the Second Amendment to allow some gun-control measures, such as restrictions on the sale of sawed-off long guns and automatic weapons.

But during the 1960s, the NRA saw gun control win wider popularity. The organization saw a danger to law-abiding gun owners and hardened its position. It saw any further gun-control laws as a limitation on constitutional rights. Executive Vice President Harlon Carter summed up the new attitude in a speech in July 1972: "Any position we took back at that time is no good, it is not valid, and it is simply not relevant to the problem that we face today. [It is] a disastrous concept . . . that evil is imputed to the sale and delivery, the possession of a certain kind of firearm, entirely apart from the good or evil intent of the man who uses it."[4]

Gun-control opponents also point out that gun-control measures discriminate against the poor and against minority communities. In fact, the only law that banned firearms possession outright was passed before the Civil War. This law targeted African-American slaves. According to T. Markus Funk,

> Early firearm laws were often enacted for the sole purpose of preventing immigrants, blacks, and other ethnic minorities from

obtaining a gun. Even today, police departments have a wide range of latitude in granting gun permits, yet they rarely issue them to the poor or to minority citizens.

The poor are often prevented from possessing a firearm even though the poor are disproportionately victims of crime. . . . Therefore any gun control measure which takes cheaper guns off the market and prevents the poor from obtaining a handgun for self-defense is arguably doubly unfair.[5]

Gun-control opponents also maintain that handguns have provided a crucial measure of security and safety for women. Author Naomi Wolf, in her book *Fire with Fire*, commented that:

The premise that women are helpless victims, unable to defend themselves, was entirely ignored by twelve million women who did something highly unvictimlike throughout the 1980s: they bought handguns. As violence against women reached epidemic proportions, women were not just sitting around. . . . While they looked after their families and ended their marriages, they were also teaching themselves to blow away potential assailants.[6]

Others disagree, pointing out the dangers of personal gun ownership. They use statistics to prove their point as well. In particular, they cite a study published in *The New England Journal of Medicine*. The study concluded that a gun in a private home is forty-three times more likely to harm a member of the household than a criminal. The organization Women Against Gun Violence, founded in 1994 in

California, says: "Gun manufacturers and lobbyists have targeted women in a marketing effort that exploits their fear of crime and violence. . . . The truth must be communicated to women that guns should be feared more than the intruders, and that the presence of a firearm in the home actually increases the danger to women and children."[7]

The United States and the Rest of the World

Gun-control advocates say the Second Amendment does not ensure that Americans can own any kind of weapon they want. If it did, then any ordinary citizen could keep tanks, or antiaircraft missiles, or nuclear weapons in their back yards. Most people would not want nuclear weapons in their neighborhoods, so there must be some limit to the right to bear arms.

Gun-control advocates believe that easy gun ownership poses a greater threat than the chance of tyranny. They point out that the United States has the least restrictive gun laws in the industrialized western world. They believe this has led to the many gun deaths and injuries here, which remain far higher in the United States than in Canada, Europe, or Japan.

Canada, for example, requires gun buyers to get a Firearms Acquisition Certificate (FAC). The FAC asks a series of questions on the individual's background. Two witnesses must swear to the truth of the statements made on the FAC. Gun buyers then go through a twenty-eight-day waiting period. All

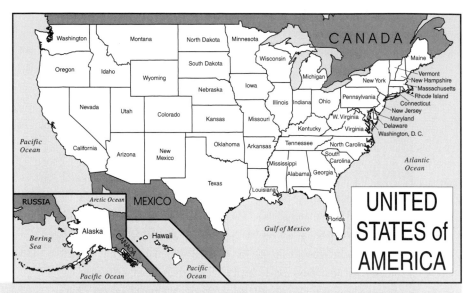

The United States has the least restrictive gun laws in the industrialized Western world.

handguns must be registered; assault weapons are banned; and the law sets a mandatory jail term for anyone using a firearm in the commission of a crime.

Other nations have reacted to gun violence with more restrictive legislation. In 1996, a gunman massacred thirty-five people in Port Arthur, Australia. After this incident, Australia banned all automatic and semiautomatic weapons as well as pump-action shotguns. The government paid cash for the weapons, and then destroyed them. In addition, Australia bans concealed weapons. All Australian gun owners must pass a written test that measures their knowledge of gun safety before getting their mandatory gun license. Although special permits for handguns can be issued, these permits are very difficult for ordinary citizens to get.

In the United Kingdom (England, Scotland, Wales, and Northern Ireland), all handguns were outlawed in 1997. This law passed after a school massacre in Dunblane, Scotland, in which a gunman killed sixteen children and a teacher.[8] Semiautomatic weapons of any kind are illegal. All citizens must have licenses to own guns of any kind, and all guns need to be registered. Those who apply for gun licenses must have no record of criminal activity, mental instability, or drug and/or alcohol abuse. They also have to give a reason for owning the gun, a safe place to store the gun, and a safe place to do target or sport shooting. Owning a gun in British cities is

Many European countries have very strict laws regulating gun ownership, among them Spain, France, and the Netherlands.

quite rare—even most police officers in the United Kingdom carry out their duties unarmed.

Other European countries also have strict gun laws. Spain bans the sale or possession of all handguns as well as automatic and semiautomatic weapons. The Netherlands generally prohibits the possession of firearms of any kind, making exceptions only for members of gun clubs. France restricts handgun purchases and allows only military personnel and certain police officers to carry them.

Other countries are more permissive. The cantons (states) of Switzerland allow their citizens to own long guns (rifles and shotguns) with few restrictions. Switzerland also maintains a national militia of men between the ages of twenty and forty-two. After going through basic training, militia members are required to keep a well-maintained assault rifle in their home at all times and to remain trained in its use. Each militia member is given a sealed box of ammunition, to be used only in the case of a national emergency. When members of the militia return for their annual term of service, militia officers inspect the box and its seal. The militia member risks a jail term if the seal is broken and/or the ammunition is missing.

Gun-control advocates may point to the low rate of gun murder in the United Kingdom and other restrictive nations as an example of the benefit of stricter gun control. Gun-control opponents point in another direction—toward Switzerland. In that country, where nearly all households keep a weapon at the ready, the gun murder rate is quite low as well, in comparison to the United States.

7

Guns and
the Future

What is really to blame for gun violence? Gun-control supporters say that the United States has too many guns, and that guns are too easy to buy. Their opponents point to a deeper social problem. They feel that American culture does not value life, that families are falling apart, and that young people do not show respect. The result is crime and violence that cannot be blamed on weapons.

During the presidential election campaign of 2000, Handgun Control, Inc., and other gun-control supporters made much of the fact that, should Republican candidate George W. Bush win the presidential election in the fall, the NRA would have a close ally in the White House. Gun-control opponents warned that Democrat Al Gore supported a photo license for every gun owner—a measure that, in their opinion, would allow the government to confiscate guns.

In a speech given in April 2000, at Fort Lee High School in New Jersey, Vice President Gore said: "One of the lessons of Columbine is that we have to stand up to the NRA and the gun industry and get guns out of the hands of people who shouldn't have them."[1]

Gore's opponent, George W. Bush, had a very different opinion. Bush did not promise any new gun laws or restrictions. Instead, he supported "character education" in the nation's public schools. Teachers would try to instill better moral values, self-respect, and regard for others in their students. This would be the best way, Bush said, to lessen violence in the schools.

The argument may have played an important role in the election's outcome. As on many other issues, voters were about evenly divided on gun control. As Election Day drew near, the NRA spent money to advertise its message against gun control, and against Al Gore. Handgun Control and other pro-gun-control groups warned about the danger of a Bush presidency, and the possible repeal of gun-control laws already on the books. The presidential vote was close, and although Gore won more popular votes, George W. Bush took an electoral vote majority and the White House.

Guns in Court

Elections are difficult to predict, and lawmakers come and go. But gun-control supporters have discovered that there is more than one way to fight their battle. While many new gun-control laws have been stopped, gun violence has brought about lawsuits against gun manufacturers. One of the first gun lawsuits was filed by James Brady, critically wounded during the attack on President Reagan. Brady sued the manufacturer of the gun that had nearly killed him, asking for $100 million in damages. Handgun Control enthusiastically endorsed Brady's lawsuit and many other civil actions against gun manufacturers.

Another such suit was brought against Intratec, the manufacturer of the TEC–9 assault pistol, which was used in a shooting spree in San Francisco in 1993. The Center to Prevent Handgun Violence, a gun-control organization, said that Intratec was selling weapons suited to mass murder and that the sale of such weapons posed grave danger to the community. Another case was brought after a boy named Kenzo Dix was accidentally shot by a friend with a 9–mm handgun in Berkeley, California. In a lawsuit that followed, Handgun Control said that the manufacturer of the gun had the ability to make the gun safer by adding devices such as trigger locks, but had not done so.

These lawsuits led to further lawsuits against gun manufacturers, holding them liable for damages. In 1998, the city of New Orleans began a lawsuit against gun manufacturers. The city, which has had a high murder rate for many years, asked the courts to hold gunmakers responsible for the costs of gun violence (many victims of gun violence must be treated at public expense). By May 2000, thirty-one cities and counties had filed suit against gun manufacturers, gun dealers, and gun trade associations.[2] In March 2000, the threat of endless lawsuits over injuries and deaths prompted Smith & Wesson, the nation's largest gun manufacturer, to strike a deal with the federal government. In this agreement, the company said it would install safety locks on its guns, among other measures, in return for protection from civil lawsuits.

New Technology

For the people of the United States, invention has often provided answers to economic and social problems. In the 1990s, gun manufacturers faced with lawsuits and calls for stricter gun control also grew inventive. They proposed a wide array of new technologies to help lower gun crime and gun accidents. These technologies included:

Trigger locks. These are simple locks placed over the trigger of a firearm. The gun cannot be operated until the user opens the lock with a small key, or enters a personal identification number (PIN). The trigger lock prevents strangers from using the gun, unless they have the key.

Voice, hand, eye, or fingerprint recognition. These technologies would allow only the legitimate owner of a gun to operate it. The gun would not fire unless the owner identified himself or herself with a thumbprint, a handprint scan, or a scan of the unique pattern of the eye retina. These new technologies have not yet been used in manufacturing guns.

Radio transmitters. In this technology, the user carries a piece of jewelry or some other small object that carries a computer chip. When the object comes close to the weapon, the weapon unlocks itself and is ready for use. These devices are already in widespread use for the unlocking of car doors, which can now be opened with a handheld device as one approaches the car.

Magnets. These devices can be attached to older guns as well as new models. The magnet is manufactured to match another magnet that is placed

One way to come up with gun control each side favors is with new technology that might prevent the use of guns by unauthorized citizens.

in the user's ring. The gun only works if the two magnets are in contact, or when the owner of the gun has his or her hand on the weapon.

Gun-control opponents point out that such new technologies will still do little to prevent guns from getting into the hands of criminals. Nor will they do anything to remove old guns from the streets or from the homes.

In addition, new technology does not solve the basic problem that gun-control measures do little to control the chain of buying and selling that can eventually place a firearm in the wrong hands. To legally acquire a weapon, a citizen has only to fill out a short form, go through a background check, and wait a certain number of days. Having the weapon, he or she can then transfer or sell it to someone else who only has to come up with the purchase price. No forms or regulations bind such private sales.

Gun-control advocates believe that private sales have brought the high rate of gun murders, suicides, and accidents in the United States. Such statistics, they say, point out a dire need for changes in the laws governing the use of firearms. Then again, it may be entirely too late to take action, as the editors of *Guns in America: A Reader* point out: ". . . it may be that gun control is a moot issue. Whatever the courts, legal scholars, or legislators decide, the inescapable fact is that there are so many guns in circulation that any attempt to assert meaningful control would require a virtual police state. No politician in his or her right mind would even seriously contemplate the effort."[3]

Other writers suggest that the United States is

growing up and away from guns, which represent a different time. As Osha Gray Davidson points out,

> As American society has become more urban, fewer professionals—including journalists—are raised and live in areas where people hunt. These city dwellers are neither familiar with firearms nor, all too often, respectful of those who are. To many journalists, just as to most other urban professionals, all gun enthusiasts are kooks unless proven otherwise.[4]

The Culture of Violence

When it comes to violence, many people believe that entertainment media also play a role. Many movies feature murders and shoot-outs. Killers and gangsters star on television shows. One popular class of video games, "first-person shooters," simply allows the player to point weapons and blast away at imaginary opponents.

In order to show their concern for widespread violence, certain stores have stopped stocking violent video games. This trend grew particularly strong after the Columbine shootings, when it was discovered that the teenage murderers were avid players of *Quake* and *Doom*. In her column, "Video Playground," *Time* staff writer Amy Dickinson reported that, "The latest versions of *Doom*, *Mortal Kombat* and *Half Life* feature realistic sound effects and depictions of violence that are close to motion-picture quality, as limbs are blown off and organs splattered. These games teach kids to connect gore and glory in a fantasy world in which the most vicious killers are the winners."[5]

The gun violence of video games prompted the creation of the Entertainment Software Rating Board (ESRB), which maintains a rating system for video games similar to the system of ratings for motion pictures. In addition, some retailers have banned certain violent video games and personal computer (PC) games from their shelves. But, as Todd Zuniga commented in *Official U.S. PlayStation* magazine in June 2000, the motivations of game-banning retailers may not always be honorable: ". . . legitimately licensed firepower-hungry patrons know that [Wal-Mart] is the safest bet for loading up with the latest .22 or a double-barreled shotgun. Wal-Mart will sell guns because they're known for it, they'll profit from it. . . . a slim stock of games doesn't hurt the bottom line and they get to snub blood-gushing game titles . . ."[6]

The Future

Will the United States ever resolve the debate over gun control? At present, the chances seem quite small. Guns remain an integral part of daily life for millions of families. A well-maintained gun does not wear out, nor is it an object that people commonly lose, throw away, or destroy. As a result, the vast American arsenal will remain in its place, the object of admiration from some and of scorn and fear from others.

The two sides of the debate seem unable to come to agreement on even the smallest detail or issue associated with guns. As Gregg Lee Carter points out in *The Gun Control Movement*:

Because the NRA has evolved a no-compromise approach to politics, there is no motivation on either side of the gun control debate to work together toward the regulation of firearms in American society, as was done in the 1930s–to–1970s era, when the NRA cooperated with various pro-gun-control legislators and other government officials. . . . What is clear is that both movements, representing the pro- and anticontrol philosophies, are now large enough and well-funded enough to take advantage of the changing winds of political opportunity and, indeed, to partly direct these winds.[7]

Supporters of gun control have made an evil hobgoblin out of the NRA and its leaders. In many instances, they have made the NRA, rather than guns and gun violence, the issue. They point out that the NRA is one of the largest and most powerful lobbying associations in the country. They assert that the NRA, by mobilizing its members in an election year, can make or break the political careers of congressmen, and that national lawmakers fear the organization like no other.

On May 14, 2000—Mother's Day—and soon after the shooting spree by Richard Scott Baumhammers, the two sides of the gun control debate gathered their forces. In Washington, D.C., a "Million Mom March" protested gun violence in the United States. The marchers called for stricter gun control, including a ban on certain kinds of weapons, safety locks on all handguns, a limitation on the number of guns that can be purchased at one time, and the creation of a national database of gun purchasers. The marchers also invited talk-show host Rosie O'Donnell to speak to the crowd. O'Donnell's views are directly opposed to those of Charlton Heston. She opposes the ownership of guns of any kind, for any reason. While Heston wants guns to be completely legal, O'Donnell wants them to be completely illegal.

The NRA ridiculed O'Donnell and the Million Mom March, and on the same day gun-control opponents put on a counterdemonstration in the streets of Washington. A group calling itself the Second Amendment Sisters held a march as well. Five women acquainted through an Internet chat room founded this group in December 1999. They saw the right to own guns as a vital and fundamental right of all U.S. citizens. They opposed any further controls on gun purchase and ownership. The Million Mom March, in their opinion, unfairly excluded their point of view.

The Million Mom March of May 2000, was passionately supported by millions of citizens—and just as passionately ridiculed by millions of others. Opponents accused the marchers of naivete and insincerity. They accused politicians who supported the march of working solely for their private gain, in seeking the votes of gun-control supporters. While march organizers sought to spark a mass movement for stricter gun-control, they knew that this event would soon be forgotten. They also realized it would be only one among many such events to be taken up, interpreted, and used as a rallying cry for those on both sides of the debate to support their point of view.

Appendix

Major Federal Gun Control Laws

National Firearms Act of 1934

Taxed the manufacture, sale, and transfer of machine guns (fully automatic firearms), sawed-off shotguns and rifles, and silencers. Required a $200 transfer tax on the sale of such weapons. Required federal registration of such weapons, and required an FBI background check, photograph, and fingerprinting of buyers of such weapons. Those owning such weapons were required to get approval of local law enforcement before bringing the weapons into a new jurisdiction.

Federal Firearms Act of 1938

Required licensing of manufacturers, dealers, and importers of firearms and of ammunition for pistols and revolvers. Prohibited sale and delivery of firearms to buyers with a criminal record.

Federal Aviation Act of 1958

Prohibited the carrying of firearms onto a passenger aircraft.

Gun Control Act of 1968

Prohibited felons, drug dealers, minors, fugitives, illegal aliens, and dishonorably discharged veterans from buying or possessing firearms. Set license fees for firearms manufacturers, importers, and dealers. Required serial numbers on all guns. Prohibited mail-order sales of firearms and ammunition. Required buyers of guns to make the purchase in their state of residence. Set a minimum age of twenty-one for buyers of handguns and eighteen for buyers of long guns.

Armed Career Criminal Act of 1984

Set a maximum fine of $10,000 for any convicted felon, dishonorably discharged veteran, or illegal alien who receives, possesses, or transports a firearm. Also fined "mental incompetents" or those who renounced their U.S. citizenship for the same act.

Firearms Owners' Protection Act of 1986

Set lower penalties for firearms dealers convicted of felonies involving sale of firearms; allowed interstate sale of long guns; set penalties for those convicted of drug trafficking while in possession of a firearm.

Law Enforcement Officers Protection Act of 1986

Banned the sale, manufacture, or importing of armor-piercing ammunition.

Brady Handgun Violence Prevention Act of 1993

Set a national five-day waiting period for transfers of handguns, with several exceptions, such as immediate need of the weapon to counter a deadly threat. Established background checks, to be effective nationwide on November 30, 1998, for purchasers of firearms. Also increased license fees for dealers.

Violent Crime Control and Law Enforcement Act of 1994

Banned nineteen different types of assault weapons; limited magazine capacity to ten rounds (but exempted all firearms owned legally before the law was passed); spent $13.45 billion for the hiring of new state and federal law enforcement officers; set life imprisonment for conviction of a third violent or drug-related crime; set the death penalty for sixty federal crimes.

Chapter Notes

Chapter 1. The Rampage

1. Jake Tapper, "The Real Culprits at Columbine," from "Salon News," salon.com Web site, <http://www.salon.com/news/feature/1999/12/30/guns/index.html> (June 2000).

2. Michael Collins and Peggy Kreimer, "Concealed Carry Law Passes First Test," *Kentucky Post*, August 20, 1999, <http://www.kypost.com/news/shoot082099.html> (May 2000).

3. Tom Diaz, *Making a Killing: The Business of Guns in America* (New York: The New Press, 1999), p. 3.

4. Earl R. Kruschke, *Gun Control: A Reference Handbook* (Santa Barbara, Calif.: ABC-CLIO, Inc., 1995), p. 183.

Chapter 2. Guns and U.S. History

1. Earl R. Kruschke, *Gun Control: A Reference Handbook* (Santa Barbara, Calif.: ABC-CLIO, Inc., 1995), pp. 72–73.

2. Jervis Anderson, *Guns in American Life* (New York: Random House, 1984), p. 53.

3. William Hosley, "Guns, Gun Culture, and the Peddling of Dreams," in Jan E. Dizard, Robert Merrill Muth, and Stephen P. Andrews, Jr., *Guns in America: A Reader* (New York: New York University Press, 1999), p. 55.

4. Anderson, p. 75.

5. Osha Gray Davidson, *Under Fire: The NRA & the Battle for Gun Control* (New York: Henry Holt & Company, 1993), p. 45.

6. Erik Larson, *Lethal Passage: The Story of a Gun* (New York: Vintage Books, 1995), pp. 198–199.

7. Andrew Stuttaford, "Andy, Get Your Gun," *National Review*, vol. 52, February 21, 2000, pp. 27–28.

8. *National Vital Statistics Reports*, vol. 48, no. 11, July 24, 2000, p. 67.

Chapter 3. The Law

1. Sam B. Warner, "The Uniform Pistol Act," *Journal of Criminal Law and Criminology*, vol. 29, p. 529 (1938), cited on Second Amendment Foundation Web site, <http://saf.org/LawReviews/Warner1.html> (January 2001).

2. Earl R. Kruschke, *Gun Control: A Reference Handbook* (Santa Barbara, Calif.: ABC-CLIO, Inc., 1995), p. 171.

3. Michael J. Sniffen, "Gun Checks Blocked 204,000 Sales," *Associated Press*, June 4, 2000.

4. Erik Larson, *Lethal Passage: The Story of a Gun* (New York: Vintage Books, 1995), pp. 211–212.

Chapter 4. The NRA and Gun Control

1. Wayne LaPierre, *Guns, Crime, and Freedom* (New York: Regnery Publishing, 1994), p. 57.

2. Osha Gray Davidson, *Under Fire: The NRA & the Battle for Gun Control* (New York: Henry Holt & Company, 1993), p. 92.

3. Josh Sugarmann, *National Rifle Association: Money, Firepower & Fear* (Bethesda, Md.: National Press Books, 1992), p. 186.

4. Statement made on *The Joey Bishop Show*, June 18, 1968, and quoted in "Charlton Heston and the Gun Control Act of 1968," from The Firearms Coalition Web site, 1998, <http://www.nealknox.com/fc/nra98/heston.html> (November 2000).

5. Charlton Heston, "Statement to the National Press Club," in Jan E. Dizard, Robert Merrill Muth, and Stephen P. Andrews, Jr., *Guns in America: A Reader* (New York: New York University Press, 1999), pp. 203–204.

Chapter 5. Gun-control Advocates

1. Gregg Lee Carter, *The Gun Control Movement* (New York: MacMillan Publishers, 1996), p. 83.

2. Sarah Brady, "Statement of Sarah Brady," in Jan E. Dizard, Robert Merrill Muth, and Stephen P. Andrews, Jr., *Guns in America: A Reader* (New York: New York University Press, 1999), pp. 207–208.

3. Osha Gray Davidson, *Under Fire: The NRA & the Battle for Gun Control* (New York: Henry Holt & Company, 1993), p. 194.

4. Earl R. Kruschke, *Gun Control: A Reference Handbook* (Santa Barbara, Calif.: ABC-CLIO, Inc., 1995), p. 201.

5. "Statement of Sarah Brady Re: Shooting at the National Zoo," April 25, 2000, from the Handgun Control, Inc. Web site, <http://www.handguncontrol.org/press/hci/042500.html> (June 2000).

Chapter 6. Gun Controversies, Old and New

1. "The Reasonable Gun Nut," interview with Michael Bellesiles by David Bowman on salon.com Web site, <http://www.salon.com/books/feature/2000/09/07/bellesiles/index.html> (November 2000).

2. James Madison, Federalist #46, from "The American Memory: The Federalist Papers," Web site <http://memory.loc.gov/home/fedpapers/fed_46.html>.

3. Denis Henigan, "Exploding the NRA's Constitutional Myth," *Legal Times*, April 22, 1991, quoted on Handgun Control, Inc., Web site, <www.handguncontrol.org> (May 2000).

4. Gregg Lee Carter, *The Gun Control Movement* (New York: MacMillan Publishers, 1996,) p. 78.

5. T. Markus Funk, "Gun Control in America: A History of Discrimination Against the Poor and Minorities," in Jan E. Dizard, Robert Merrill Muth, and Stephen P. Andrews, Jr., *Guns in America: A Reader* (New York: New York University Press, 1999), p. 391.

6. Naomi Wolf, *Fire with Fire: The New Female Power and How to Use It* (New York: Random House, 1993), p. 216.

7. Undated statement from Women Against Gun Violence Web site, <http://www.wagv.org/women.htm> (June 2000).

8. Tom Diaz, *Making a Killing: The Business of Guns in America* (New York: The New Press, 1999), p. 8.

Chapter 7. Guns and the Future

1. From "On Anniversary of Columbine Shootings, Bush and Gore link Gun Control to Character," April 20, 2000, allpolitics.com, from CNN.com Web site, <http://www.cnn.com/2000/ALLPOLITICS/stories/04/20/campaign.school/index.html> (July 2000).

2. From "Victory in the Courts," Handgun Control, Inc. Web site, May 16, 2000, <http://www.handguncontrol.org/press/cphv/051600.html> (June 2000).

3. Jan E. Dizard, et al., "The Rise of Gun Culture in America," Introduction from *Guns in America: A Reader* (New York: New York University Press, 1999), p. 6.

4. Osha Gray Davidson, *Under Fire: The NRA & the Battle for Gun Control* (New York: Henry Holt & Company, 1993), p. 168.

5. Amy Dickinson, "Video Playground," *Time*, May 7, 2000, p. B30.

6. Todd Zuniga, *Official U.S. PlayStation* magazine, June 2000, p. 50.

7. Gregg Lee Carter, *The Gun Control Movement* (New York: MacMillan Publishers, 1996), p. 111.

Glossary

amendment—A change or addition in law or in a state or federal constitution. The first ten amendments of the United States Constitution are commonly known as the Bill of Rights.

armor-piercing bullets—Bullets coated with teflon or some other substance that allows them to easily penetrate metal barriers or body armor.

assault weapons—Military weapons designed for higher speed, accuracy, and/or ammunition capacity, which first reached the civilian gun market in the 1980s.

automatic weapon—A gun that fires multiple rounds with a single pull of the trigger.

background checks—A computer search for a past criminal record. By the federal law known as the Brady Bill, background checks are done on all individuals seeking to purchase handguns from licensed gun dealers.

concealed carry laws—Laws that allow ordinary citizens to apply for permits to carry concealed handguns.

derringer—A small and easily concealed handgun, common in the late nineteenth and early twentieth century.

gun buy-backs—Also known as turn-in programs, in which citizens give up their weapons to local police for cash or some other benefit.

gun license—A permit that allows an individual to buy and own a gun.

gun registration—A written record of a particular gun's sale and/or ownership.

machine guns—Automatic weapons sharply restricted by federal law in 1934.

militia—A military unit made up of armed civilians.

plastic guns—Weapons made up partially of plastic or some other non-metal material, which allow the weapons to pass unseen through weapons-detecting devices.

revolver—A handgun that fires bullets from a revolving chamber, allowing the user to fire more rapidly than is possible with single-shot rifles and muskets.

Saturday Night Specials—Inexpensive handguns that became widely available in urban areas of the United States in the 1960s.

sawed-off shotgun—A long gun whose barrel has been cut in order to make the weapon easy to hide and carry.

semiautomatic—A gun that reloads automatically after each pull of the trigger.

straw purchase—Buying a weapon for another individual who may not be legally entitled to buy or own the weapon.

trigger locks—Devices placed over the trigger of a gun, which prevent the gun from being fired without first being unlocked with a key.

waiting period—A period of time, which varies by state, required before a buyer can take possession of a purchased weapon.

Further Reading

Dolan, Edward F. and Margaret M. Scariano. *Guns in the United States*. New York: Franklin Watts, 1994.

Gottfried, Ted. *Gun Control: Public Safety and the Right to Bear Arms*. Brookfield, Conn.: Millbrook Press, 1993.

Murray, James M. *Fifty Things You Can Do About Guns*. San Francisco: Robert D. Reed, 1994.

Kim, Henny, ed. *Gun and Violence*. San Diego: Greenhaven Press, 1999.

Miller, Maryann. *Working Together against Gun Violence*. New York: Rosen Publishing Group, 1997.

Roleff, Tamara, ed. *Gun Control: Opposing Viewpoints*. San Diego: Greenhaven Press, 1997.

Schulson, Rachel. *Guns: What You Should Know*. Morton Grove, Ill.: A. Whitman, 1997.

Schleifer, Jay. *Everything You Need to Know About Weapons in School and at Home*. New York: Rosen Publishing Group, 1993.

Schwarz, Ted. *Kids and Guns: The History, The Present, The Dangers, and The Remedies*. New York: Franklin Watts, 1999.

Weir, William. *A Well Regulated Militia: The Battle over Gun Control*. North Haven, Conn.: Shoe String Press, 1997.

Internet Addresses

Brady Campaign to Prevent Gun Violence
<http://www.bradycampaign.org/>

> Pro-gun-control site, carrying news and information on pending legislation, congressional voting records, gun industry lawsuits, press releases, updates, and petitions. Promotes local activism on the part of members and visitors to the site.

Gun Owners of America
<http://www.gunowners.org>

> Calls itself "The Only No-Compromise Gun Lobby in Washington," in the words of supporter Representative Ron Paul of Texas. Emphasizes legislative action and reaction. Carries legislative alerts, pro-gun ratings of congressional representatives, and analysis of pending legislation.

National Rifle Association
<http://www.mynra.org>

> National lobbying and educational organization dedicated to gun rights and opposed to further restrictions on gun ownership. Video updates, information on pending legislation on state and federal levels, educational programs, online firearms museum, notable speeches, press

releases, "fax alerts," and information for hunters and sport shooters.

Second Amendment Foundation
<http://www.saf.org>

Emphasizes opposition to gun-control legislation on constitutional grounds. Carries editorials and articles on legal aspects of court cases and laws relevant to gun control. Also provides educational and legal programs on the meaning and interpretation of the Second Amendment.

Violence Policy Center
<http://www.vpc.org>

Dedicated to reducing gun violence and to increasing gun control. Publishes fact sheets and statistics, news updates, state laws, legislative information, and policy issues.

Index